GREAT COMMERCIAL DISASTERS

In this series

Great Operatic Disasters
Hugh Vickers

GREAT COMMERCIAL DISASTERS

STEPHEN WINKWORTH

Illustrated by Michael ffolkes

Introduction by Sir Peter Parker

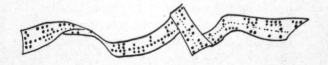

M

ISBN 0 333 32277 0

First published 1980 by
MACMILLAN LONDON LIMITED
4 Little Essex Street London WC2R 3LF
and Basingstoke

Reprinted before publication

First published 1981 by
PAPERMAC
a division of Macmillan Publishers Limited
London and Basingstoke

Associated companies in Auckland, Dallas,
Delhi, Dublin, Hong Kong, Johannesburg,
Lagos, Manzini, Melbourne, Nairobi,
New York, Singapore, Tokyo, Washington
and Zaria

Printed in Great Britain by
BUTLER & TANNER LTD
Frome and London

To the Reader

May your luck be better!

INTRODUCTION

Few of us would want to press a claim to be experienced or even expert in commercial disasters. Yet most of us relish them – of course, not the kind which leaves widows weeping and orphans penniless, or men out of work. Oh yes, there is a gasping fascination in the really juicy disaster: the big bang of self-blown, overweening business arrogance, or the inspired but ultimately self-destructive ingenuity on the part of some entrepreneur who finally disappears up his own market. Or – even more conducive to glee along the corridors of corporate power – some pompous organisation falling flat on its interface of public relations.

For all those interested in the world of money – wealth-creation is the acceptable, heavy-breathing way to put it these days – such events are the spice of life and a theme of awesome relevance. There, but for the grace of good luck, judgment, above all humour, go ... well ... quite a few successful but close-shaven members of the business community.

I am convinced that a sense of humour is about the only thing that will sabotage disaster when business grows to a certain scale. So thank goodness Stephen Winkworth has had the wit to get together, and Michael ffolkes to illustrate, some of the most amusing of commercial disasters for a more enduring posterity than they enjoy as ephemera on the floor of the world's Stock Exchanges. These sagas I find dauntingly instructive and yet a relief in a way. There is no doubt about them – Stephen Winkworth has given them their due – their full-scale definition as downright fiascos. At least we know where we are – right down there, in the flaming red, on the bottom line.

Of course, I personally am conscious these days of so many other ways of commerce failing disastrously; but in

7

stealthier, slower motion than some of these all-dancing, all-wailing spectaculars brilliantly produced in this entertaining book of industruction.

For instance, just consider the disastrous advance of bureaucracy in business: it is like a kind of corporate Dutch Elm disease, killing off the life in organisational trees in so many giant companies. Then there is the sheer brute force of the language of commerce. I do not mean simply the rubbishy 'being in receipt of yours of the inst. and ult.', or the almost unbreakably coded jargon of business schools, but beyond all that, the gross scale of the promoter's style.

The commercial disaster of the language goes further than advertising copy. We have come to take for granted the humourlessness of reports about industrial action – which means not working. For my part, since being railroaded, I find I live with 'Chaos'. With twenty thousand trains running a day, railwaymen are acquainted with grief, and human fallibility is daily in the headlines. We have an open day every day. But, more often than not, any minor incident is Rail Chaos. There seems little in between no news bliss and Rail Chaos – except possibly Fares Shock.

But these are creeping, crawling commercial disasters, not Winkworthy: he tells sad stories of the deaths of king-sized, he-management, of the real big ones that didn't get away. And I am cheered by two reflections in this merry evidence of commercial doom.

First, some disasters move in a mysterious way to the good: some disasters seem a rehearsal for a future success. Concorde: all right, in the short term it's the rich what gets the pleasure, and the poor what gets the bags. But it has proved that there is a business market that wants supersonic travel – it will come, and will make the world smaller, perhaps even friendlier for that matter. Isambard Kingdom Brunel is another heroic example of the ambiguity of some disasters. He strained himself to death over his last epic venture launching that great liner: yet the world gained from his Great Eastern promise. Alas, his Great Western promise was lost: Brunel's large-gauge railway, his 7 ft vision, was beaten – but I wish the world had it now.

Secondly, this book puts us on warning: do you sincerely want to avoid a rich disaster? If so:

– Don't be first, not absolutely first

– Don't be Super; think big but don't grow bigheaded

– Don't stop laughing

This book should help.

July 1980   Peter Parker

'... from his left lapel.'

How to arrive at the office,
by Onassis and Niarchos

AWKWARD things sometimes happen on the way to the office – the sprint for the train resulting in the split trouser, the unanticipated lamp-post resulting in the black eye, or the passing vehicle which by adroit interaction with a puddle sprays the garments with effluvia.

Perhaps the worst recorded disaster of this kind occurred to those two great men of commerce Stavros Niarchos and Aristotle Onassis, who were returning to New York in one of George Baker's twin-float executive seaplanes early in 1954. This method of transport enabled them to land on the East River, not a stone's throw from their Madison Avenue shipping offices. It is, one has to admit, a cut above the usual combination of airports and taxis, let alone the 8.10 train or the No. 11 bus which is the lot of us humbler mortals. The disadvantage of these beautiful machines, beloved of aviation buffs since Schneider Trophy days, is that they are unusually allergic to logs. Floating logs lurk in abundance in the East River, and on the occasion I have in mind a particularly vicious one inflicted severe damage on the aircraft's starboard pontoon. This resulted in an immediate deviation from a relatively straight path through the water to a relatively circular one. After a couple of circles, the little party drifting further downstream each time, the pilot decided on drastic action to prevent them being carried right out to sea beyond hope of rescue.

'You'll have to climb out on to the port wingtip' he shouted above the roar of the Pratt and Whitney engine, 'it's the only way to lift the float out of the water enough to straighten her up.'

The two millionaires, with the audacity of their race, lost no time in scrambling out of the cockpit and along to the very tip of the wing. A dab of throttle, the starboard float emerged from the water with great suddenness, and the air-

11

craft bounded forward – shedding its wingtip load in the process. The East River in 1954 was not a good place to go bathing. Logs were not the only things which floated down it into the great cleansing ocean, and when the two gentlemen arrived, dripping, at their offices, they were given a wide berth.

The life of a tycoon is full of hardship, but it does seem doubly cruel to Onassis that he should have arrived in this repellent state when he was already in bad odour in another sense with the American Government. Twelve of his T-2 ships, worth over $1 million apiece, were under distraint on the grounds that he had bought them from the U.S. Government through a company fraudulently claiming to be American controlled. A member of the firm who had advised him on the legality of the original purchase, Herbert A. Brownell Jr, was now Attorney-General. This is just one of those ironies which regularly afflict the rich and powerful: you hire lawyers one day to give advice and the week after a member becomes Attorney-General and tries to put you in jail.

Onassis and the Vanishing Ink

IN SUCH a predicament as I have just described, even the knowledge that you still have another hundred million or so in the piggy bank is not really any consolation. Courage, and the conviction that you are in the right, is essential to the tycoon's make up, but he must also be a very wary fellow. The Greek epithet 'polymetis', formerly applied to Odysseus, and meaning 'multifariously devious and cunning' about sums it up.

Just about at the same time that Onassis received his ducking in East River, along with Niarchos, tides and crosscurrents of history were gathering into a series of whirlpools in which the polymetic Onassis suffered several bites from the jaws of sharks.

The notorious Saudi-Arabian oil-tanker deal is recorded history. The circumstances surrounding its signature belong to a more shadowy region, and though the following story is accepted as true among other shipowners, it would be impossible, short of an interview in the Elysian fields, to discover exactly what happened.

This is how I imagine it. Onassis emerges, dripping, from the East River, thumps a spluttering Niarchos on the back and removes a piece of seaweed from his left lapel.

'Thanks, old chum, you saved my life.'

'Any time, Ari, any time.'

They proceed to the shipping office, where a suitable exchange of clothing is effected.

'Ari, old fellow, I gather things are a bit tough for you right now, with the Attorney-General trying to clap you in the clink. Sure there's nothing I can do?'

'No, no, my dear Stavros. A spot of belt-tightening should see me through. I'll go easy on the caviar. My love to Eugenie.'

'And mine to Tina.'

In this exchange of pleasantries, Onassis was in fact playing his cards very close to his face, for awaiting him in his office was a fellow-countryman who had for some months been pursuing him through Monte Carlo and Paris with a very big deal indeed. The essence of this deal was that Onassis should supply Ibn Saud with his own oil-tanker fleet, on a completely exclusive basis. This was a new idea, since the oil producing countries had not so far attempted to own the means of transport for their oil, and they relied on various arrangements with oil companies (who mostly belonged to a fearsome conglomerate called ARAMCO), which in turn contracted the transport to shipowners, who mostly consisted of Niarchos. Onassis did not have many of these contracts at that time, so his move, though excellent strategy from his own point of view, might well have looked a trifle damaging to the interests of his beloved brother-in-law. Nor of course would ARAMCO have welcomed with open arms the prospect of being cut out of a very large slice of the market.

The fellow-countryman awaiting him in the office was a go-between, a man of extraordinary talent whose remarkable career culminated in the Saudi-Arabian deal.

'Well, now your lawyers have dealt with the contract, Mr Onassis, I think it's time for the signature. Hope you changed lawyers after the T-2 business, eh?'

This pleasantry did not go down particularly well.

'I will sign but it must be counter-signed and ratified by Ibn Saud within forty-eight hours or the deal's off, do you understand?'

'Naturally, Mr Onassis. You have my word.'

Onassis gave a grunt. He had the fellow's word!

'And anyway I'm not signing until this evening.'

'That's all right: six o'clock? Good. Always such a pleasure to do business with you, Mr Onassis. Oh, by the way, I saw Mr Niarchos just now on my way in. Looking very fit nowadays, isn't he?'

'Yes, I believe he does a lot of swimming. Goodbye.'

The middleman was shown out of the room. An Odyssean look passed over the face of the great man. He summoned his secretary.

'What have you done with the suit I arrived in?'

'We left it in a bucket of detergent, sir.'

'Well iron it, bring it up to my office, and call me a cab.'

'But it's in a terrible state, sir.'

'Never mind, just do as I say.'

Half an hour later a shabby looking figure wearing dark glasses got out of a cab on the corner of Times Square and slipped into a little shop bearing the legend 'The Magic Box – Jokes, Tricks and Novelties'.

A secret transaction then took place – a purchase with which no aide, however loyal, could have been entrusted.

There is no way of guessing what the middleman would

'*... slipped into a little shop*'

have done with the agreement if he had not been successful
in obtaining Ibn Saud's assent in Riyadh thirty-six hours
later. Nor what powerful pressures he would have been able
to exert with this explosive document after its ratification.
Nor is there any record of the expression on his face when
he noticed that just after both parties had signed, Onassis's
signature had mysteriously, magically vanished away.

The vanishing ink did not in fact save Onassis from the
eventual wrath of ARAMCO, though no doubt it afforded
a temporary protection against immediate dangers. A boy-
cott ensued. During this time he was said to be losing
£17,000 a day. The closure of the Suez canal in 1956 however
found Onassis in an excellent position. Other owners' ships
were by this time all fully contracted long-term at poor rates,
and Onassis's boycotted craft were able to step in and pick
up the plums.

Disastrous Names I

AN AUSTRALIAN airline really made things hard for itself by choosing to adopt the name 'Emu' – an Australian bird, granted, but a *flightless* one: small wonder they did not prosper. The following story was told to me concerning Emu Airways, over a few cans of Foster's lager. A regular passenger of the airline, living in Melbourne, was a blind lady in her sixties who always travelled with her guide-dog. The guide-dog, a fine golden Labrador, was much loved by the flight crew, and it used to occupy a separate seat beside the lady passenger. On one occasion the aircraft had to wait for half an hour or so for some transfer passengers, and the dog became restless. The lady summoned the stewardess and explained that she would like to take him outside for a little walk. The captain overheard the conversation and volunteered to go himself. The sun was dazzling outside, so he put on a pair of sunglasses. Just as he was emerging from the aircraft, with his four-stripe pilot's uniform, dark glasses, and a guide-dog in a harness, the transfer passengers arrived in their bus, took one look at their captain ... and got back in again.

For French nationals the name chosen by a private Egyptian airline – MISair (pronounce it in French and it means 'misery') – was scarcely the most propitious. French airline passengers were, however, really alarmed by the slogan '——vous ouvre les portes du Paradis', though the promise that the doors which were to open led to Paradise and not the other place encouraged some sinners to try their luck. Shortly after this a number of tragic crashes occurred involving luggage-bay doors opening in flight. Realising at last how appropriate their slogan had been, the airline in question rapidly dropped it. Another appropriate slogan may be seen to this day on a wall flanking the road into Buenos Aires from the airport 'Par——vous y seriez déja' (With——you'd be there already). The irony here is that the wall is that of the cemetery.

Reminder of a Lifetime

W HAT IS the mechanical equivalent of an over-zealous suitor? A story which has been going round for many years in the offices of the Addressograph-Multigraph Corporation of Los Angeles concerns an unfortunate inhabitant of Alberta, Canada – let us call him Albert Abel – who was a subscriber to *Time* Magazine. As Edward Spielman, Addressograph-Multigraph's Manager of Special Activities, put it to me, this may be one of those stories which gets embellished with each telling, or it may be one hundred per cent true.

During the early nineteen-fifties Time Inc. decided to install a new system for sending out subscription reminders, and AM Corporation was called in. A modern machine was installed which addressed and franked the cards and prepared them for despatch in mailbags, all in one operation, without human intervention. There were several hundred thousand names on the card index, and the machine worked busily for a number of hours, filling fifteen mailbags which were duly collected by the Post Office for sorting and delivery.

I do not envy Albert Abel. To be the object of unwanted female attraction would be one thing: the attentions of a machine are altogether more terrifying. Especially when its *billets-doux* are delivered by the sackful – fifteen sacks full in this instance. There was room for no one else in its heart, evidently. Fairly soon there was room for no one else in Mr Abel's front hallway. Wise man, he capitulated. If they wanted him to renew his subscription that badly, he could not find it in his heart to refuse. The hallway was so blocked that he couldn't get out to send a letter, so he sent *Time* a telegram: 'O.K. I GIVE IN.'

The Great Fur Mix-up

MOST stories about commercial disasters among the retail trade involve a shop or store losing money as a result of error or dishonesty, whether perpetrated by staff or by customers. Once upon a time, in a large department store, things happened very much the other way about. Since the story is about the fallibility of memory, it is not to be wondered at if memory takes its revenge against all who try to tell it. There are many versions of the tale, and needless to say it is vehemently denied by each shop it is told about.

Let us imagine then a busy Saturday evening. A thick stack of cheques and account debits lay on the till box which was at that moment being locked ready for despatch to the Accounts Department. Displays were being covered up and counter tops polished.

The tall willowy blonde who swept in at that moment had one of those faces which once seen is never forgotten. The assistant in the Fur Department had certainly seen her before. She was one of the 'smart set'.

Was she too late, she wondered? It was about the wild mink stole – she needed it for tonight as they were going to the gala opening of the opera season. No, no, the assistant replied, they *had* just locked the till, but of course it would be all right. Boxes, tissue paper and silk ribbons were produced in a flash, and the assistant, who was something of an opera enthusiast himself, chatted merrily as he did up the beautiful, expensive parcel.

It was not until Monday morning that the manager of the Fur Department, who had returned from a weekend break, asked who had bought the wild mink stole. This was when the argument began. Was it the wife of the Chairman of Bashforth Steel? Was it that model, the Duke of Cheltenham's friend? Well, where was the sales slip? Where indeed! It was too late for recriminations about this error in routine. Confusion grew upon confusion. Was the Duke of Cheltenham still alive, and had not the lady in question been seen lately with a certain well-known actor? The accounts department was summoned to a hasty consultation. Their lists only made matters worse. The lady fitted the description of so many of their most valued customers. In any case the bill was surely not for the lady herself, but for – well, whoever it was that paid her bills. Any attempt to find out who this was would be impossibly embarrassing, and ruin the store's reputation for discretion.

The Accounts Department withdrew to commune with itself. Eventually it was decided that to write off the cost of the mink stole was not an option, in view of the appalling example of irresponsibility it would set for the staff. To wait for the lady to return was equally out of the question: how would they know it was her? The reputation of the firm would hardly be improved by allowing the error to be broadcast among the clients. No, the only thing to do was to bill all fifty-two of the store's most important customers, who had wives or lady-friends fitting the description of that familiar yet tantalisingly unidentifiable face. The Accounts Department would be ready to issue letters of profuse apology to all fifty-one who were unjustly billed.

The term *embarras de richesses* might have been coined specifically for the Fur Department that year, and the thought of the end of season profits still brings a blush to their cheeks. Twenty-nine of their most valued customers paid for that one mink stole, and it is not known to this day which was the lucky lady.

The Smart Aussie

A REMARKABLE incident occurred at a fashionable London jeweller. The year was 1932. The customer in this case was an Australian, accompanied by a beautiful French girl. The object of their choice was a plain diamond solitaire ring, not as big as the Ritz, nor yet as small as the eye of a needle. The French girl, whose name was Dupont, had slipped the ring onto the fourth finger of her left hand and was eyeing it and her cavalier with equal amounts of covetousness and delight.

'You are paying by cheque, sir? Very good, I will have the ring delivered to you as soon as the cheque is cleared, if you will be so good as to tell me your address.'

'Now look here, every shop in London town that's any good knows my name – Jack Phillips. And you can ask Claridge's Hotel if my credit's sound. If you think you're going to take my ring off Miss Dupont's finger ...'

'Of course, of course sir. We have to be so careful in our profession you know. Perhaps you would wait just one moment....'

The sentence trailed off as the manager disappeared into the back room. The Australian customer waited impatiently, drumming his fingers on the glass counter, while the necessary enquiries were made.

'An Australian gentleman, tall and very strikingly dressed, with a scar in the shape of an exclamation mark on its side just above his right eyebrow. Yes, thank you Mr Turnbull. And how is Mr Asser's asthma, if I may ask? Good! Ah, Mr Asprey – a little matter of credit. I wonder if you have come across a Mr Phillips from Australia: banks with Glyn's. Yes, he is rather a card, isn't he? But you say he's as solid as malachite. Well, you would know, Mr Asprey ...'

'Ah, Mr Phillips – I must apologise for this little formality. Next time you call on us we shall not need to be so difficult, sir. But you know how it is. No, one can't be too careful

'. . . *drumming his fingers on the glass counter*'

these days, mademoiselle. Will you be needing a cab, sir? The doorman will attend to it. I am so glad the ring was to your taste.'

Later that evening, as he was preparing to leave the shop, the jeweller received a telephone call from the Chief Accountant at Claridge's.

'That Australian gentleman you were asking about, sir. I thought I should tell you. He left rather hurriedly just now. On his way to Croydon aerodrome. No, there's no forwarding address.'

The jeweller did some swift thinking. He had smelled a rat right from the start: honest people don't put themselves in Mr Phillips's position, and if they do ask for credit of some kind they don't adopt that hectoring manner. Vine Street Police Station, with which he was on excellent terms, was straightway alerted, and before very long he was speeding towards Croydon in a six-cylinder Wolseley car, together with three beefy officers. Stern measures, perhaps; nevertheless the ring was worth at least £3,000, and he feared he was being taken for a ride (and he detested puns). The Wolseley screeched to a halt on the apron of Croydon aerodrome.

A de Havilland Dragon Rapide biplane was standing on the runway, its engines racing under the arc-lamps. 'Yes, that's the Paris 'plane' (the apostrophe was barely audible above the din).

A furiously protesting Mr Phillips was bundled down the gangway and into the police room near the control tower.

'You'll be hearing from my attorneys about this,' shouted Phillips, black with rage but with a nasty triumphant look in the eye with the exclamation-mark scar.

'And your bankers will be hearing from me', retorted the jeweller stoutly. Miss Dupont's reaction to this exchange is not recorded: no doubt it was tearful.

The incident was later said to have caused much satisfaction among certain sporting acquaintances of Mr Phillips. As for the jeweller, he was left to reflect, when the Glyn Mills cheque was honoured the next day, that the profit on the sale of a £3,000 ring does not go very far towards settling a £50,000 suit for defamation.

'Yes, that's the Paris 'plane.'

Bourne's Super Order

COMMERCE is essentially all about the interchange of goods and valuables on the basis of mutual understanding. A break in the lines of communication is apt to cause disaster.

In Bourne & Hollingsworth's emporium in London's Oxford Street in the nineteen-seventies there was a foreign lady buyer in the knitwear department. The lady in question had a good fashion sense and an eye for a well-made product, so when she visited the Knitwear Fair in Milan with Edward Bourne, a young Director of the store, her comments were highly critical. It was not a good year, as they both agreed. Before flying on Bourne instructed her to place a relatively modest order: 'Four to five thousand pounds' worth of the sweaters, and the rest pro rata.' She nodded agreement and made a note of the amount, leaving Bourne to make his way out of the crowded exhibition hall to catch his plane.

Some weeks later, the order began to arrive. 'Really, Mr Bourne, there are not very good arrangements for storing in this department. Already we have run out of space and there are still two more van-loads to be delivered.'

'Van-loads of what?'

'Why, of the Italian knitwear order, Mr Bourne.'

'But that can't take up very much space, surely? What do you mean, van-loads?'

'Mr Bourne, the skirts alone already have taken up the whole space. Then there is the children's knitwear, and the sweaters – well, it is not possible to store forty-five thousand pounds' worth of sweaters in this little space.'

It is easy to see how the words 'four to five' had become 'forty-five' over the hubbub of a hall packed with highly vocal Italians. It was too late to rectify the mistake, and there were a lot of amazing knitwear bargains in the Bourne & Hollingsworth annual Christmas Sale that year.

The Poet and the Salmon

BUYING mistakes, even on this scale, rarely damage the fortunes of a large department store, but they can be much more serious for an individual. The poet and publisher James Michie, who was living at the time in Cornwall Gardens in London, decided one day to order some smoked salmon for a luncheon *à deux* with a lady friend. This was in the gracious fifties, when it was still possible for a poet of modest means to ring Harrods Food Halls at eleven o'clock with a small order and confidently expect delivery in time for lunch. The salmon was to be the main feature of the meal, along with some chilled white wine and thinly sliced buttered brown bread, so Michie wanted to be sure there would be no shortage. 'I would like to order some smoked salmon – lots of it – enough for two hungry people.'

It was the smell, more than anything, which made that lunch so memorable. The wooden trays started to arrive at half-past twelve, borne by three Harrods delivery men.

'Well, it says 'ere smoked salmon, Mr Michie, two hundred portions, Cornwall Gardens.' By the time the necessary remonstrations and telephone calls had been made, the salmon had lain, lightly covered and oozing in its trays, stacked like a pagoda in the hall, for thirty odoriferous minutes.

The damage which this sort of misunderstanding – two hungry people, however hungry, could scarcely have coped with two hundred portions – is liable to inflict on the normal workings of commerce can only be imagined.

'. . . enough for two hungry people.'

The Berry Book Bonanza

'A POET and his money are soon parted' it is said, though I am assured that it was not as a result of the salmon incident that Mr Michie was compelled to spend the best years of his life translating Horace and Martial. Nevertheless, poetry and commerce do not generally go hand in hand, and one should not be surprised if a poet, entrusted with an extraordinary commercial asset, treats it in a highly bizarre fashion.

The poet Harry Crosby, an American living in Paris in the twenties, was surrounded by enormous wealth. There was his uncle John Pierpont Morgan (the man who lent France two billion dollars in 1924 to strengthen the franc, under the Dawes Plan). There was his wife Caresse, born a Peabody – the shipping family, one of the members of which, George Peabody, founded the Peabody Trust to house the poor of London. There was another most remarkable uncle, Walter van Rensselaer Berry, friend of Henry James and mentor of Edith Wharton, who had spent a lifetime and a not inconsiderable fortune on amassing one of the most impressive collections of antiquarian books of the age.

Harry Crosby, having started life working in one of uncle Jack's banks, decided like T. S. Eliot that a poet in a bank was something of an anomaly. Crosby's poetic talents were expressed more in his lifestyle than in his written work. The lifestyle included a Bugatti, a black greyhound with gold toenails called Clitoris, a great deal of champagne, orgies, opium and a mystical identification with the sun – a symbolically black sun which signified death.

While Crosby was somewhat in awe of his uncle J. P. Morgan he grew to find his book-collecting uncle Walter Berry more in tune with the tastes of an emerging poet. It must have been difficult to live up to two such exceptional men, and the aloof, commanding features of the great book-collector staring at posterity from among his crammed shelves do not look like those of a man who would have had much time for his nephew's extravaganzas. Nevertheless it is clear that he was fond of the boy in his dusty way, and when he died he left the bulk of the collection to Harry. Edith Wharton was not particularly pleased with this arrangement, but her reaction when she discovered how Harry was treating the inheritance must have been electrifying.

The ten thousand or so volumes, from the earliest incunabula to works from the collections of Madame de Pompadour and Le Roi Soleil, illuminated medieval psalms and Persian miniatures, were piled into the Crosby apartment, filling every room from floor to ceiling – including the nursery of his little step-daughter Polly. With poetic simplicity, Crosby decided that the thing to do with all these books was to read them. Having read them, he would concentrate their essence, rather in the way that heavy water used to be manufactured, by a sort of distilling process. At the end he would be left with the one truly valuable book, containing the wisdom and poetry of the ages, and by a further process of reduction, he would find in that book the one word symbolising the essence of life.

This involved ridding himself of the remaining 9,999 – or thereabouts. It should be remembered that these books were valuable enough for his uncle to have employed a permanent armed guard for their sole protection. So his behaviour must seem all the more extraordinary, and from a sordidly commercial point of view, disastrous. For the technique he hit upon was this: every day he would fill a pillow-case with a few dozen of the rejects from the previous evening's 'distillation' and make his way down to the Seine. Along the banks of the Seine there are open-air stalls piled with second-hand books. Generally scorned by the rare-book snobs, these stalls are a useful place to pick up an old Maigret or a German grammar, and just occasionally a slightly rarer book nestles among the scruffy heaps.

Leaning, with the pillow-case full of books behind his back, over the booksellers' tables, he would furtively slip a

'*Departure ... in triumphant style.*'

sixteenth-century calf-bound Herbal or a signed first edition by Voltaire, with a price neatly pre-pencilled in the fly-leaf (say Fr. 5 for the Herbal and Fr. 7.50 for the Voltaire), in amongst the old school-books and the second-hand Guides to Brussels. He would then retreat to the nearest bridge and watch the ensuing comedy: A shuffling collector would approach and run listless fingers over the junk. Convulsive jerk as fingers close round unbelievable treasure. Look of amazement as collector opens Fuchs' *De Historia Stirpium*, Cologne, 1545, priced at Fr. 6. Negotiations with astonished stall-holder. Protestations and counting of money. Departure of collector in triumphant style, a shuffler no more.

The entire collection was gradually dispersed, mostly in this way. Of course, Crosby's reasons for behaving in this unconventional manner with his assets were not principally to obtain the voyeuristic pleasure of witnessing their discovery. He was making an existential statement. It was a poet's assertion of the Christian attitude towards material possessions. Thus what might seem to be a commercial disaster from an accountant's point of view can in fact be a poetic triumph. It would be a fine tribute to the existential spirit if this book were made the passive, objective symbol for a re-enactment of this poetic triumph.

Of Lucre and Lucifers

WHILE HARRY Crosby was giving away a fortune in books, and his uncle was lending money at eight per cent to the Government of France, another financial operator on the gargantuan scale was casting his net over the world. J. P. Morgan was in fact the only big banker who did not succumb to that sinister Swede, Ivar Kreuger. But he lost the battle of the French loan, for Kreuger stepped in with $75 million at five per cent, in 1927, when Morgan would lend no more.

There have been massive bankruptcies and huge financial empires built on shifting sands, but never has there been fraud on so far-reaching a scale, or so brilliantly executed, as that of the Match King.

Lucifers, as they used to call them, were the substance of Kreuger's empire. At his peak, the matches of three-quarters of the world were produced under his control. This was the basis of a vast empire, reaching out into financial operations of deep and mysterious complexity. So complex indeed were the fantastic paper palaces of credit and currency that accountants Price Waterhouse in their final investigations were never able to unravel the last ramifications of the structure. Kreuger was the Piranesi of finance.

How this was done, on a superficial level, is not hard to understand. He relied first of all on the unquestioning obedience of his employees, whether they were accountants or the managers of his many dummy banks in Holland, Liechtenstein and elsewhere. Secondly, he grasped, like the directors of Equity Funding, the simple principle that what the investor wants is (a) a fat dividend, and (b) a robust balance sheet. The first he managed to go on paying out until the very end, using the Ponzi principle of paying from capital when true dividends were lacking. The second he never had any trouble with, since he composed the documents himself and instructed his managers and accountants to sign. He was able to do this because of the cloak of mystery in which he surrounded all his actions. Such was the commanding presence of the man, and such was his isolation from the rest of humanity, that any doubts were quelled by the feeling that 'I.K.' must be right, for he was to all intents omniscient.

But such interpretations of Kreuger's success are simplistic. He was to the last degree unusual, even awe-inspiring, in both abilities and habits. His memory was superhuman: he could quote the movements of every share on the New York Stock Exchange over the past twenty years. He hoodwinked Governments, he even fooled Maynard Keynes, who praised him unreservedly for his role in the Hague Conference of 1930, when he helped set up the Young Loan to Germany, paying $30 million from his own pocket. He had, too, some very weird tastes.

Let us imagine a day in the diary of Kreuger the Superfinancier, at home in Stockholm:

'Another night in Stockholm penthouse hideaway. Make note of name of girl and rate her performance B2 in black book.

Swedish exercises, then let myself out through steel doors with triple lock, closing them with master key. Door sticks, catch little finger. Must have it mended (the finger).

Climb into 60 mph speedboat and zoom off to Island Match Palace.

Frugal breakfast: rolled oats with grated apple followed by spiders' eggs again.

Write balance sheets for accountants to sign, then draft instructions to open new Dutch Bank.

Ring my brokers in New York (the fools!) Say hello, then nothing at all for 17 minutes (my silences always shake them rigid). Order them to make new $10 million issue of Kreuger & Toll 'B' Shares. Glad I invented 'B' Share idea – one of my ripest.

Retreat to Silence Room: stay silent for usual 30 minutes; then order another one thousand lilies of the valley for regular requirements.

Terrify two new accountants: give them usual contract with clause for $25,000 fine for desertion.

Frugal lunch: turbots' eyes with grated carrot, *pommes allumettes*, Monte Carlo pudding.

Retire to library. Read elegant scientific article by Dr Lemoine on *Treponema pallidum* found by darkfield illuminator in tears of syphilitic child (Mercy Hospital Clinic). Collate later MSS. on life of Charles XII.

Meeting with Director of Bank of Sweden (the dunderhead!). Make him guarantee new issue of International Match Corporation. Demonstrate my mechanical peacock for him, and the little jumping pig with rolling eyes. He is transfixed. Quote details of five principal loans he has made that morning, and chide him for not being tougher. He is flabbergasted. Press hidden contact under desk which makes my phone ring, and show him out. While away rest of weary afternoon, making multi-million dollar deals with Spain and Japan.

Buy golf club in Chile. Order stone Cupid for fountain, Park Avenue penthouse. Arrange to play red light on it, so it looks as though it's spouting blood – nice touch.

Pack valise with silk stockings and gold lighters from regular stocks in drawer and indent for replacements. Then off to Berlin for night of pleasure.

Arrive, change into workman's clothes, and set off for usual dive. Pass wretched match girl in rags. Show her silk stockings, then buy her stock of matches with 500 Mark note (a special dud from my collection: only printed one side. Ha, ha, ha, ha!). Same old crowd in dive – Norris, Isherwood & Co. He looks at me but doesn't register: so much for *I Am a Camera*. Drink six working men under the table. Catch five a.m. train to Paris, to pick up Grand Cross of Legion of Honour. At the ceremony I leave off all my other decorations, and only wear Stockholm Olympic Medal. This slays them with my modesty (the suckers!).'

The above would have been a normal day's work for Kreuger around 1930. He shot himself a couple of years later. That was when the Final Contract became due. Which contract? Well, by this time it should be obvious: principal characteristics – infallible memory, insensitivity to pain, soft clammy look, fascination with syphilis, beautiful voice. washes his hands a lot, buys cartloads full of lilies of the valley – what does it all add up to? Remembering the fact that the empire is based on *Lucifers*.... Students of Thomas Mann's version of the Faust legend will have guessed already.

Two final facts clinch the Kreuger enigma. For a start, he had a particularly dreadful sense of humour. One instance of this is his behaviour to the poor match-seller. Ilya Ehrenburg's *United Front* relates a similar incident, obviously referring to Kreuger, and this was the book he was found with in a pool of blood in his Paris flat. Another instance was his answer to the New York journalist who asked him if he was thinking of marrying an American girl:

'No, I prefer a Swedish Match.'

Ye gods and little fishes, that was what the great funster, the Swedish arch-swindler, actually said! Did no one sell their shares in IMCO or Kreuger & Toll on the spot? On the contrary, they all fell about laughing and said 'he has a human side after all!'.

'Human side' or no, Kreuger had an Achilles heel, and the world seems to have been amazingly blind at not recognising it. This was his morbid dread of head waiters. He was once so terrified by the head waiter of Maxim's in Paris that he dared not ask for a ham sandwich and ordered Lobster Thermidor, champagne, ice cream *and a ham sandwich*.

Faust of course felt just the same. For it is a well known fact that head waiters can see right through to your soul, and if you have hocked that vital organ to the Head Waiter of the Nether Regions, the man in the tail coat with the charming demeanour who greets you as you step through the swing doors need only give one glance to see the emptiness within. That is why Ivar Kreuger could not look them in the eye.

It is a sad reflection that the whole collapse of the Kreuger empire, with its tidal waves of bankruptcies and its dire implications for the years of the Depression, could have been avoided by the simple deployment of one head waiter, strategically placed.

'... one head waiter, strategically placed.'

The Shell Demolition Mystery

TO RETURN to the theme of 'failures in communication', it was presumably some verbal confusion which lay at the root of the following incident, recounted by Michael Ivens, Director of Aims.

The words 'Shell' and 'Esso' are after all almost indistinguishable, especially if pronounced in a strong brogue in an Irish bar. In the 1950s Esso closed down most of their bulk plants and cut their distributing costs by having bigger plants and bigger vehicles distributing over a wider area.

For reasons of convenient access, Esso and Shell plants were very often sited next to each other, along canals, rivers or railway sidings. On one occasion in Ireland the message went out for a small Esso plant to be demolished over the weekend. Through the natural verbal confusion to which I have alluded, the contractors knocked the Shell plant down instead. Shell had not scheduled it for demolition, and they were not very pleased.

Mr Ivens suggests that if competition is taken to its extreme conclusion, deliberate failures of communication could be used to demolish the opposition.

United Nations Efforts for Peas

THE BIBLICAL example of the Tower of Babel should be forever in the minds of those who work for, or are employed by, the international civil service.

In one case an entire five-year crop replication trial was carried out by a United Nations team of experts on the sweet-pea, in Northern Thailand. It was not until the reports of the $750,000 project reached headquarters that a furious administrator discovered the mistake. In a conference with three colleagues – an Indian, a Frenchman and a Thai – the administrator vented his anger.

'I told them *peas*, goddammit, peas for protein! They can't eat the flipping flower.'

To which his Indian colleague replied: 'On the contrary, sir, in my country it is a very normal occurrence to make flour from the chick-pea. It is *besan*, the chick-pea flour, very nourishing, very palatable.'

At which point it seemed a good moment to break for tea. Of course it is very difficult to avoid this sort of incident. The alternative would be to encumber working procedures with cross-checks and controls to the point where the efficiency normally associated with civil service becomes virtually unattainable.

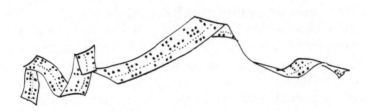

The Sardine Standard

THE MAIN problem besetting international civil servants in their dealings with commerce is that the two sides are playing different games. One side is trying to win promotion, or avoid falling asleep; the other is trying to make a profit.

When it comes to dispensing international aid, the idea is that funds, or perhaps tractors, have to leave the donor organisation and find their way into the recipient country. There are those in the recipient country whose job it is to ensure that the money does reach them, without being in some way lost or squandered on the way. In parts of the world where communications are poor, and there are more guns than policemen, these officials cannot afford to allow the money to leave their immediate vicinity. Their sense of duty compels them to keep a very firm grip on it and protect it from loss, frequently by salting it away in a Swiss Bank.

In South-East Asia shortly after the end of World War II a most equable method was evolved of distributing aid to the needy through normal commercial channels; yet to this day it is labelled a 'disaster' in U.N. circles. An international welfare agency was concerned with improving nutritional standards among the islanders scattered through the archipelagos of the Philippines. For many of these people the war had meant an immediate confrontation with twentieth-century horrors – the bombardment of beaches, the arrival of foreign troops, the occupation of villages and the destruction of crops. For others it had meant trade with the new arrivals, replacing older patterns of exchange, and in some cases the destruction of traditional trading routes. As all such simple fish and coconut economies are as frail as the craft in which they are transacted, many of these people were 'living at or below economic subsistence levels and suffering nutritional deprivation' – which means they were beginning to starve.

The agency found that emergency supplies of fish protein, in an easily transportable form, were essential to supplement

38

their diet until life returned to normal. Several tons of tinned sardines were accordingly procured and flown out in a Sikorsky S-42 flying-boat, together with a small team of men who distributed them fairly among the island population. Unfortunately for this well-meaning plan the islanders were unfamiliar with the concept of tinned food. Scarcely any were literate either, though even if they had been able to read it would hardly have helped, since the printing on the tins was in Russian. On one side of the boxes there was a smiling Caspian fisherwoman with a shawl, while on the other a pair of crudely drawn fish chased each other, nose to tail.

Even the most sophisticated devotee of tinned food would agree that the sardine tin occasionally defeats their efforts. It is not a tin for a beginner. But for the islanders the problem never arose, since it was plain to them from the labels that the tins were sacred objects: did they not depict on one side a Western Goddess, and on the other the symbol of the Yin and Yang of the Fish God? Little coconut-palm shrines were built, and the white men's offerings were placed in them. Life returned to its familiar routine of fishing and harvesting coconuts.

Some months later a genial Philippine trader happened to come upon one of these coconut-palm shrines. He heard the extraordinary story of the flying-boat, and the men in strange white clothes. He decided that this was an occasion for commercial *savoir-faire*. In exchange for a few sacks of rice and a few bales of cloth he was able to repossess the entire consignment of tins, which he transported to his warehouse in Manila.

Shortly after this the trader, a well-connected man, heard from a friend that tenders were being invited for supplies to continue the welfare agency's nutritional programme. All truly great commercial ideas are simple: what could be easier than to submit a tender to the agency's headquarters for the exact amount of tinned sardines required, f.o.b. Manila? Not only was the price quoted lower than any other tender re-

'... white men's offerings were placed in them.'

ceived, but the goods were actually immediately available to the agency at Manila, an advantage no rival could offer.

Thus it was that a new element was introduced into the seasonal pattern of the islanders' life. Every spring the sacred boxes would arrive, to be carefully stored in the little coconut-palm shrines until the coming of the trader, with his gifts of bales of cloth and sacks of rice. And the islanders grew to love the white-suited men in their big winged boat, and their hearts warmed to the good trader. The trader likewise was, as can be imagined, happy with the arrangement. The welfare agency was delighted with the smooth progress of their nutritional aid programme. Experts who visited the islanders reported an improvement in their well-being. They were better dressed – a good indicator in primitive economies of a situation of nutritional surplus. An extension of the original five-year programme was ordered from Geneva.

It was not until the seventh year of the programme that problems began to occur. Quite simply, the basis of the simple economic cycle set in motion by the welfare agency was beginning to deteriorate. The original cartons had rotted away. The tins had started to rust. Many of them had burst. The numbers of viable cartons remaining had fallen well below the agency's quota.

What followed was a microcosm of deflation in action: the decay of a currency in its most literal form. As the supplies of the basis of exchange – the precious tins – rapidly diminished, the primer of the economic pump (the welfare agency) made enquiries, the wholesaler whose genius had made the system work disappeared without trace, the islanders lost their annual bounty, and recriminations flew in Geneva. And all because of rust. What an argument for a return to the gold standard.

The Swiss Credit Racket

ENGLAND is undoubtedly the place for the new world banking centre. It has always seemed to me that Switzerland, with its mountains and lakes and quaint old towns, is a most unsuitable repository for money. It makes the place too expensive for the tourist. London, on the other hand, has vast areas of depressingly dreary territory within easy reach of the City, on which banks of every size and shape could well be built.

One cannot imagine the Italians making the same mistake as the Swiss, and cluttering the shores of Lake Garda with international banks and institutions such as abound in Geneva. Indeed, at those points where Italy and Switzerland have common borders there have in recent years been several signs that the Italian attitude to money is being exported. If this goes on the Gnomes, with their pompous probity and hypocritical reticence, will take flight. British financial whizz-kids can then take over in London and give OPM – that magical commodity, Other People's Money – a proper chance.

A promising incident occurred in April 1977 at Chiasso – the name by the way means 'racket' or 'din', with a strong overtone of 'infernal confusion'. One Ernesto Kuhrmeier, the chief manager of the local branch of the Credit Suisse itself, devised a fascinating method of 'Italianising' the Swiss banking system and arranging for Italian depositors to obtain Swiss Francs in exchange for Lire.

During the years 1974–77 the Lira lost about 50 per cent of its value compared to the Swiss Franc, so one sympathises with the Italian desire to exchange Lire for Swiss Francs. It is illegal of course, but when did mere law ever hamper the Italian spirit? The Swiss are unfriendly toward Italian advances of this nature, discouraging them by various odious methods, including ten per cent negative interest per quarter on all sums over Sw. Fr. 100,000, 35 per cent withholding tax on the interest on Swiss bonds, and a generally unwelcoming demeanour towards Italians with suitcases full of 10,000 Lire notes.

It was revealed that the kind Kuhrmeier had over the years quietly channelled Sw. Fr. 2,170 million into a company based in Vaduz, Leichtenstein, called Texon Finanzanstalt, which itself lent money to various Italian firms, thus completing the circle. Had it not been for the misfortune that the Italian firms lost most of the money on various hare-brained schemes (Sw. Fr. 30 million were lost on one project alone, to build luxury bungalows at Albarella Mare, near Venice) the philanthropic system would doubtless have continued to operate for many more happy years.

To be sure of being able to supervise the system personally, Kuhrmeier would adopt an aggressive stance towards other bankers. He is reported as having said 'Don't try to get into business in Milan: there I am king.' He would issue nervous customers with hand-written guarantees on official Credit Suisse paper. In all some thousand or so Italians appear to have benefited.

Owing to Texon's losses, of nearly Sw. Fr. 2.2 billion, (about $900 million), the President of Credit Suisse Management was forced to resign, while Kuhrmeier was cruelly imprisoned in Lugano.

Meanwhile the Swiss banking establishment, with the usual lack of sensitivity to public relations displayed by banks on such occasions, offered to support Credit Suisse. Dramatically, at midnight on 26 April standby credit of Sw. Fr. 3 billion was announced by a consortium consisting of the Swiss National Bank, the Swiss Banking Corporation and the Union Bank of Switzerland. The shares of Credit Suisse fell from Sw. Fr. 2,780 to 2,000.

As a leading financial commentator remarked at the time, midnight offers of standby credit are not calculated to dispel the idea that a bank is in trouble. And why limit it to Sw. Fr. 3 billion?

Bank of England Lets Out Cork

IT WAS the height of the secondary banking crisis of the early seventies. The Bank of England was conducting urgent talks to set up the 'lifeboat' system, designed to prevent a collapse of secondary banking pulling down some of the major circulating banks as well.

Present at these discussions was Sir Kenneth Cork, senior partner of Cork, Gully & Co., the chartered accountants. Cork, Gully & Co. is the principal firm of company liquidators in the City of London and Sir Kenneth, who was Lord Mayor of London in 1979, is a familiar presence at any well-conducted company dissolution.

It was two o'clock in the morning and the great iron doors clanged to one after another. As Sir Kenneth was shown out by the Wicket Gate, 'for heaven's sake', said the senior official, 'pull down your hat and put up your collar! If *you're* seen leaving *here* at this time of night the pound won't stand much chance tomorrow.'

'It was two o'clock in the morning . . .'

The Colonel of the Nuts

THE LANCASTER bomber circled Dar-es-Salaam early in 1947 and the whole town stopped work. It was the biggest aeroplane they had ever seen. Within it was the advance party of the biggest planning disaster the world had ever seen. The inhabitants of Dar-es-Salaam were not to know that at the time, of course. But they soon realised that something was afoot which would 'upset their cosy corner and put up the price of gin', as James Cameron expressed it.

What put up the price of gin was nuts. Millions of nuts – *Arachis hypogaea*, known until then as monkey nuts, but dignified, for parliamentary reasons, with the name that clung to them ever afterwards – groundnuts. Unfortunately most of the millions of nuts remained either in the ground or in the head of Mr John Strachey, Minister of Food.

I was fortunate enough to meet, in the bar of a private hotel near Cheltenham, a Colonel who was a member of the little band which pioneered the whole venture. My informant prefers not to give his name, in fact he says he was always one for keeping a low profile.

'Fact is, I doubt if any of the chaps would remember me today. Well, here goes.

'I don't want to boast of course, but our advance party consisted of as fine a bunch of men as you'd have found in Africa since Monty left the Western Desert. There were fellows among them who had driven bulldozers under fire. There was a scientific chappie with an amazing tea-strainer contraption and a few bits of litmus paper for the soil recce. There was a super guy with a great big moustache and a jolly grin, who came from Cheshire – like the cheese, get it? Not quite sure what he was doing, but a great guy to have around. Then there was a real white hunter fellow, because after all the bush where we were going to grow the nuts was pretty well virgin territory, apart from a few natives of course – and we didn't want any trouble with them. Besides there

46

might be beasties around – you wanted someone who knew whether to wait till he saw the whites of their eyes.

'The white hunter led the way, in his big slouch hat with the leopard-skin band, and his python-skin belt with his belly hanging out over his shorts. Great big fellow with a lot of foliage on the upper lip. Camp was pitched at Sagara, by a stream, with sausages roasting in the old kerosene tins.

'As it turned out, Sagara was no go for the permanent base camp, which was rather a shame as it was a decent sort of place with running water and waterfalls and what not. The trouble was, the natives – Africans, that is – used to water their livestock there, and the white hunter reckoned it would cause trouble if we moved in. Then one of those super things happened – don't put this down old chap, don't want to tell tales out of school* – which sounds like an awful shemozzle but all turned out O.K. in the end: the chaps discovered these bottles of shampers in the mess stores and got well and truly stinko. Next thing they drove into a mess tent. Well, fair do's, no names no pack drill, but before long they were heading out for Kongwa, a whole convoy of jeeps. Started off like a sort of procession, African boys waving palms, lanterns swinging, some sort of chant going on in the background. Well, it was Stanley country, you know. He was pretty well the last white man there. Anyway, they were carrying one of the chaps on a sort of litter, and three or four more of them brought up the rear, carrying the last crate of shampers. Some of the jeeps got stuck, or the chaps driving them dozed off, but the leading jeep jammed his gear into four-wheel drive and went careering off into the middle of this jolly marsh. I don't know if you've ever driven a jeep in action – no, no, never apologise old chap – but there's not much that can stop a jeep in four-wheel drive, and somehow we

* Lest the reader should conclude that the author is a rotter, it should be pointed out that a remarkably similar account is contained in *The Groundnut Affair* by Alan Wood (Bodley Head, 1950)

got through that marsh with nothing to steer by except a light of some sort that was burning in Kongwa (wretched little place before we moved in of course). Well, believe it or not old chap, that track we made is now the Sagara-Kongwa by-pass!

'Anyhow, the way we saw it was this: we'd won the war, and we had all these damn great 'dozers and modern scientific equipment, and hang it, farming is just a matter of digging a few trenches and scattering seeds and stuff when you come right down to it. So, we reckoned if there was anyone who could show the world how to grow groundnuts it was us.'

Contemporary photographs show the tractors assembled in military formation for the assault on the bush. My informant at this point became quite maudlin about what splendid chaps they all were and how super it was when the 'dozers and tractors smashed through all the beastly bush leaving smooth ground with proper trenches and windows, but he refused to discuss the later stages of the project.

'Trouble was, they all lost their nerve: the government, the contractors, half of them were a lot of wets.'

I am inclined to think he was being a little hard on the human element. The real culprit was Nature. Nature put up a very determined fight against the scheme from the start. In a war there is always a good deal of chaos and confusion, because people are suddenly given new and unfamiliar jobs and there's no telling what they may have to do next. Mistakes are made: efficiency is less than perfect. But against this the other side is human too, and making similar or even greater mistakes. Nature does not make mistakes, nor does she yield to frontal attack. She is inexorable.

Nature's weapons in the groundnut war included soil that became iron hard and broke tungsten carbide rakes and ploughs; six-inch scorpions; swarms of 'killer' bees which attacked tractor drivers; small pox; water with the same taste and effect as Epsom salts; tsetse fly; the buffalo bean – a climbing nettle propagated by wind-blown pods; and various forms of wild-life and game. At one point trace-cutting was brought almost to a halt by what could only be described as an Elephants' Drinking Club. This had regular hours, which most unfortunately clashed with the working hours of the trace-cutting English. The elephants would trail solemnly to the rock crevice to drink their fill, one after the other, and then trail solemnly back again, occupying the hours from 3 p.m. to 6 a.m. The elephants knew what they were doing. As the advance party was soon to find out, the worst and ultimately crushing weapon deployed by Nature was drought.

Man's weapons included 200 gigantic ex-U.S. Army tractors from the Philippines. Scheduled to arrive in February 1947, they actually reached Kongwa in August, two-thirds of them breaking down either on arrival or immediately afterwards. Unfortunately no one had thought they might need overhauling. By the end of the year they had all broken down.

Dismayed at this failure, John Wakefield, whose report had so impressed Strachey in 1946, thought up the idea which symbolised the whole scheme: swords into plough-shares. Sherman tanks were converted by Vickers Armstrong into giant tractors. 580 'Shervicks' were sent out. Such was the eagerness which characterised the scheme that no one had thought of sending a few out for trials first. They all had to be modified to make them usable under African conditions. A more successful innovation was chain-clearing, evolved later in the scheme. Two tractors pulled the ends of a 160-ft long anchor chain, tearing up large trees and bushes in a most satisfying manner, leaving the trunks all facing in the same direction. It was found possible to clear forty acres a day like this.

Man's final weapon was himself – 2,000 English men and women, and about 30,000 Africans. It is a measure of the disastrous failure of the scheme that eventually these Africans, many of whom had left their farms to work for the English, began to starve. The scheme did not even produce enough to feed its own workers, let alone the world's hungry millions. Another chilling thought is that more groundnuts were bought as seed than were ever harvested.

Throughout, the project was marked by a constant reduction of targets. Originally, in the Wakefield Report, three and a quarter million acres were to be cleared. It was hoped to clear 150,000 by the end of 1947. As month by month the actual achievement fell pathetically short of the targets (one thousand acres by June, ten thousand by the end of August, another two thousand by October) the spirit of optimism remained, and no one could bear to face the truth, which was that Nature was going to win. Finally that first year, 7,500 acres were planted in place of the hoped-for 150,000. The 'more realistic' target set for the following year was 60,000 acres, still far beyond what was possible. And the capital cost originally estimated at £24 million for the whole scheme, had gone over £50 million. Meanwhile Strachey was talking in Parliament of his 'hard-headed' business approach, and while admitting that costs had gone up, still referred vaguely to 'a really large acreage running into millions'.

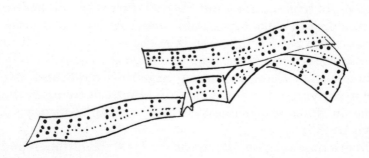

Rubber Bands

PROJECTS on the scale of the Groundnuts Scheme are rare; but just as the best endeavours of the scientific, military and agricultural brains of a whole country can be defeated by attempting to jump from the familiar to the gargantuan scale, so in lesser projects a sudden expansion is invariably fatal.

A resident of Cape Town shortly after the war discovered a need, found a cheap and ingenious way of filling it, and made himself into a rich man. The need was for rubber bands, which the inventive African mind found invaluable for a host of purposes from constructing huts to holding pieces of machinery together, hobbling goats, completing an elaborate coiffeur, making catapults, as well as more familiar uses. The method of manufacture was to obtain from the nearest ex-Army dump as many old inner tubes as possible, and slice them up into rings – instant rubber bands.

Having worked at this useful trade for a number of years, and having amassed the usual outward symbols of wealth – the Land-Rover, the fine house in the hills, the private Cessna – the rubber-band merchant was persuaded by his European friends to invest his profits in 'real' rubber-band manufacture.

It is only too sadly obvious, in retrospect, that the processes of large-scale industrial production had nothing in common with the ingenuity and flexibility of the original method. But what could the unfortunate man have done? He had the money to buy machinery, he had the contacts and techniques for selling the product, and the original source of raw material – the inner tubes – was rapidly dwindling. As can be expected, there were problems in finding trained mechanics to look after the production machinery, there were breakdowns and failures in the supply of spare parts, heat affected the stored rubber, dust got into vital control mechanisms, scorpions lodged in the pile of finished bands, and, more important than all these factors, the price was too high for the majority of African purchasers.

51

Learning from this tragic example, I have hit upon an updated, and so far as I can see foolproof, improvement uniquely suited to the urban jungle of London. This source of rubber bands involves even less manufacturing than the inner-tube variety. It will not have escaped the attentive pavement watcher in England's major cities that a new windfall crop has recently begun to appear among the sweet-wrappers and doggies' little messages with which we are more familiar. This is the Post Office Rubber Band Windfall.

Ever since the great day (recorded by Bernard Levin in *The Times*) of the Post Office 9,000,000 gross rubber band deal, wherever there are two or three letters gathered together on a joint trip to the same destination, a free rubber band goes along for the ride. This rubber band is usually allowed to fall in the hallway or on the pavement when the letters are collected. If the reader observes, after school hours, a troupe (I hesitate to say 'band') of small boys progressing rapidly but methodically through the streets of London, their eyes glued to the ground, stooping occasionally to seize the windfall bands in special tongs and thrust them into their shoulder bags, he will be able to recognise the origins of another great commercial enterprise, which the author is currently organising, of which details may be obtained from S. Winkworth, Esq., c/o Macmillan London Ltd., Little Essex Street, London W.C.2.

The Clever Tailor

ANOTHER timely idea which depended on the chances of post-war surplus was the brain-child of an East End tailor. The hard part of the scheme must have been to secure the ex-Army trucks, which in 1945 were still in great demand both inside and outside the Army, and the petrol to drive them. Having achieved this, the tailor located a surplus which no one else had been able to think of a use for: black-out material. Windows and skylights of factories and homes throughout the country had been draped in this material for the past five years, so there was a lot of it available, and it was largely in very second-hand condition.

During his military service in Aden the tailor had taken an informed sartorial interest in the clothes worn by the local populace. He had also made friends and contacts in Cairo. He had promised to get in touch when the war was over, and though it was not quite over yet, the end was now in sight. He alerted his contacts to expect delivery of 100,000 black burnouses, in three weeks' time.

The burnous is a simple garment compared to a three-piece suit, and by a clever use of cutting machinery and a pool of unemployed seamstresses, they could be turned out, from the blackout material, for next to nothing.

£95,000 was the gross profit of those three weeks' work. Casting about for other opportune methods of bridging the gap between supply and demand, the tailor then hit upon an Army dump of worn-out uniforms, which was destined for disposal. In this case he was able to buy his raw material for less than nothing, since the Army actually paid him to clear the rubbish away. But what could the uniforms possibly be used for? He would think of something. Meanwhile it looked too good a bargain to miss.

As he was driving back from the dump with a truckload full of frayed and tattered cloth, the truck had a puncture. It was a hot and sunny September afternoon, and as he struggled with the heavy tyre he dropped it onto the un-protected toe of his sandalled foot. Howling in agony he managed, nevertheless, to hoist the punctured tyre onto the tyre bracket from which he had taken the spare. He noticed it was badly worn. He would have to get another, and the cost of that, plus the petrol, would about equal what he had been paid for disposing of the pile of uniforms. He began to wish he had stayed in his tailor's shop in the Old Kent Road instead of taking the day off on this unlikely errand.

Stopping at the Army Depot where he had obtained the truck, he ran into an old friend. 'I'm going to need a new tyre for this heap,' he said. 'Looks as though you'll be needing new tyres all round, the state they're in. I say, what have you done to your toe?' (The injured limb was turning bright purple, and the tailor was limping piteously.) 'Comes of wearing sandals, you sloppy civvy! Why can't you wear proper boots like the rest of us.' He paused to demonstrate the worthiness of boots by kicking a pile of old tyres.

'... *a vital nerve in the brain.*'

'Oh, it's a habit I picked up in Aden, I suppose.' Just at this moment, a particular twinge from the toe connected with a vital nerve in the brain. Tyres were another thing which when used had a negative value ... Cloth, tyres, sandals. ... Aden.

Sandals made from old tyres with cloth straps are to be seen to this day in many parts of Africa and the Middle East.

Once again, the idea proved to be a gold-mine: the raw materials were free, the cost of manufacture tiny, and this time the market was even larger, and the supplies available in almost limitless quantities.

The accumulation of capital, and success, are dangerous to the pioneer, and, as in the case of the rubber-band merchant, the tailor was tempted to formalise his position and set up as a 'proper' manufacturer of clothing. The virtues of inventive opportunism which had served him so well initially became a positive liability when confronted with the complexities of industrial life, the raising of capital, and financial transactions west of Eastcheap. The end of the story is too sad to dwell on, but needless to say it involves the Bankruptcy Courts, and in the end a return to retail sales – this time, of Army Surplus Goods and Equipment, back in the Old Kent Road.

The Lagos Cement Blockage

IN 1974 the Nigerian Ministry of Defence decided on a major expansion of its facilities and infrastructure. Under General Gowon's Third National Development Plan it was decided to embark on a full-scale construction programme involving new roads, airfields, barracks and military buildings of all sorts. Someone worked out that this would require a great deal of cement. Whoever that person was, I do not envy his lot during 1974 and 1975, because clearly he made one of the biggest floaters of all time.

What he seems to have failed to work out was that the arrival of these enormous quantities of cement – some twenty million tons in all – would necessitate an enormous amount of unloading. As the maximum unloading capacity of the port was only 2,000 tons per day, someone should have tried multiplying that figure by the number of days in a year, and he would quickly have noticed that twenty million tons were going to take twenty-seven years to unload. Allowing for the rainy season, which knocks about a third off the available days for cement unloading, the figure increases to a round, Biblical forty years.

The Nigerians did their best. It proved an expensive exercise, since a ship waiting to unload its cargo has to be paid demurrage, at the rate of $4,100 a day in this instance. By October 1975 there were 400 ships, all authorised by the Government, from such places as Roumania, Greece, Spain and Britain, waiting inside, outside and in the general environs of Lagos Harbour. Port Harcourt and Port Wani were also doing a brisk trade, and eventually an unloading rate of around 1.4 million tons per year was reached. The main problem was the lack of silos. All the cement had to arrive in bags, and even though a system of unloading at buoys into bulk carriers was developed, the ports remained completely blocked with ships. Other goods had to be imported by road, and two rival enterprising teams of long-distance lorries were

56

quickly organised. The German one became known as the Afrika Corps, though out of tact the British refrained from calling theirs the Eighth Army.

As one British executive put it: 'I rather think military minds got their sums wrong, and having got them wrong failed to appreciate that if you have a five-year plan you don't need all your materials in the first year. Actually I rather wonder where they are going to keep all this cement. It rains a lot in West Africa and I'm afraid that does cement no good at all.'

It must have been a miserable business for the crews of the cement ships. For a start, they were not allowed to go ashore, as the strong currents around the harbour made the passage of tenders extremely hazardous. Two Chinese crew members were drowned when their tender capsized. Communications with the shore were terrible, and there was a beer and cigarette famine. Any merchant seaman who survived a year of isolation under these conditions, while the owner of his ship became a millionaire from demurrage charges, deserves some pretty hefty compensation.

The last word should perhaps go to the Lagos *Sunday Times:*

'The only constructive course is for the Government to calculate how many ships it can use within the next six months and tell the rest to dump their lousy cement in the Atlantic Ocean and go away, now!'

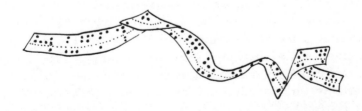

The Airship Panic

THERE IS a tradition of periodic excesses of national excitement, such as that which led Lord John Russell to raise the income tax from sevenpence to a shilling in the pound in 1848, the French Invasion Panic of 1861, the clamour stirred up by the *Pall Mall Gazette* in 1844, the Dreadnought Panic of 1910 and the Airship Panic of 1913. More recent excesses have included the Biggest Airliner Panic of 1949 and the Supersonic Airliner Panic of the 1970's.

At such times, national pride is at stake, though the average Englishman does not take much interest in the proceedings, beyond protesting feebly when his taxes are raised. Nevertheless the ability of politicians and the press to stir each other up into states of righteous nationalism is clearly demonstrated.

The Airship Panic, while directed with some justification towards the Hun, who appeared to be the source of these terrifying objects, was otherwise indistinguishable from the Flying Saucer epidemic. Huge and sinister shapes were seen moving over the Yorkshire moors at night, displaying red and green lights. On closer examination the airships turned out to be the planet Venus, or a flock of birds, or similar airship-shaped natural phenomena. The connection between flying saucers and the tax-payer has yet to be made, but eventually its time will come.

'This nation must make provision to defend itself from these alien visitors ... these Powers which have the Capacity and the Will to crush our land with one blow. A great building programme must be launched, with flying-saucer assembly lines at Portsmouth and garages for the great machines at Cardington.' I hear already the speeches at Conservative dinners, the leaders in the *Daily Express*. When that moment comes, readers of *Great Commercial Disasters* WILL BE READY.

A first bold attempt to stem the Airship Panic was made

in 1909, with the construction of His Majesty's Airship No. 1, aptly named the *Mayfly*, which cost the taxpayer £35,000. This was built by Vickers, who were chosen because of their knowledge of submarines. The only flaw in this argument was that while submarines are intended in the main to go *down*, airships are generally intended to go *up*, and this the *Mayfly* was unable to do. Not that there was anything small-minded or hesitating about the design: she was over 500 ft long, and must have looked a splendid sight as she braved the elements, moored to her mast at Barrow. For a long time Vickers wisely refrained from letting her do anything else. After all, they had achieved the object of the exercise, which was to prove that we British could build an airship as well as the Germans. Then, alas, they were tempted to lighten her structure, which resulted in her breaking in half. A gust of wind hit her amidships as she was being pulled out of her covered dock, and that was too much for her.

R100 – R101

THE TAX-PAYER's next chance to shine came in 1929 under Ramsay MacDonald. As Brigadier-General Lord Thomson of Cardington, Secretary of State for Air, put it in a speech at the time:

'People are always asking me to give a name to R101. I hope it will make its reputation with *that* name.'

The reputation R101 did make for its name could scarcely have been the one he intended. Lord Thomson lost his life a year later when R101 crashed at Beauvais on her maiden flight.

There was a rival airship being built at the same time by Vickers. As Nevil Shute's autobiography *Slide Rule* explains, the new Vickers team bore no resemblance to the 'idiots' who constructed the ill-fated *Mayfly*. (That is what Rear-Admiral Sturdee called the *Mayfly's* designer at the Court of Enquiry.)

The rival, the R100, was designed by our greatest engineer, Barnes Wallis, and his Chief Calculator, slide rule at the ready, was Nevil Shute himself. It was really unfair to the Government team that the other side had all the geniuses. But Vickers had some pretty stiff problems to cope with too, including the locally recruited female labour: 'The girls were an eye-opener ... uncouth, filthy in appearance and habits ... incredibly foul-mouthed ... promiscuous intercourse was going on merrily in every dark corner ... problems we had not contemplated when we started to build an airship.'

An official directive which both teams had to cope with was the Airworthiness of Airships Panel's decree that the German system of attaching the gasbags to the airship's girders was not to be used. Barnes Wallis, being a genius, simply invented geodetic construction, which solved the problem with supreme elegance, and came in handy later when it came to designing the Wellington bomber. The Government team used an elaborate cat's cradle of wires to hold the gas-bags, and when these had to be let out later in a desperate attempt to get enough lift, not only did the bags lurch sickeningly about inside the outer covering, but they chafed against the bolts and other horrible sharp projections which stuck out in all directions.

Lift was always the weak point of the R101. The trouble lay in her heavy engines. It was firmly believed at the time that petrol engines were unsafe in the tropics, so five colossally heavy railway diesels were used. Or rather, four were used. The fifth was left idle throughout the flight, being intended only to give reverse thrust when mooring, as the team were unable to produce a reversing propellor. When it became obvious that R101 was not going to have enough lift, they cut her in half and stuck in an extra section.

That all these peculiarities did not add up to a sound flying machine did not matter, since the certification was done by the Air Ministry, and they were hardly likely to refuse a Certificate of Airworthiness to their own baby.

R100, the capitalist airship, was completely successful, proving its abilities by flying to Canada and other places. Once after a transatlantic crossing an engineer found his watch, which he had taken off while working on a top girder, still safely balanced on her outer hull. This did nothing to redeem her, and the idea of using airships to communicate with the far-flung outposts of empire was dropped.

Before going on to consider some of the other great flagships of the air built at taxpayers' expense, it is worth recalling Nevil Shute's comments on R101:

'The disaster was the product of the system, rather than of the men themselves .... It was impossible for them to admit mistakes without incurring discredit far exceeding their deserts, for everybody makes mistakes from time to time. Surely no engineers were ever placed in so unhappy a position.' The directors of capitalist industry, on the other hand, '. . . prevent the engineers they employ from taking on work that is beyond their powers . . . they do this by virtue of their own long industrial experience, which enables them to assess the difficulty of the job and to engage staff suitable to do it. The men at Cardington had no comparable restraint . . . the civil servants and politicians above them . . . were quite unfit to exercise that type of control.

'I am very willing to recognise the good in many men of these two classes, but a politician or a civil servant is still to me an arrogant fool till he is proved otherwise.'

The Beautiful Brabazon

I WONDER whether Nevil Shute retained the healthy sceptical sentiments just quoted when Bristol started work a dozen years later on the largest aeroplane in the world: the Bristol Brabazon.

The project was exciting enough to stir the blood of any aviation enthusiast. The objective was, as in the case of the airships, to link the far-flung corners of Empire, and the air-craft was built to use the short runways of remote airfields in Africa and the Far East. It had to combine colossal range with a low landing and take-off speed. There was a contradic-tion between these two requirements, the first of which would be met by a very big aircraft, and the second by a very small one. The designers got round this by making the Brabazon very big but very slow. The structure was made as light as possible, and the wing was made so thick that a grown man could walk about inside it. This gave enormous lift at low speeds, but enormous drag at higher ones.

The result was a sort of monstrous powered glider, with a maximum cruising speed of 250 m.p.h., landing speed of 100 m.p.h., take-off at 85 m.p.h. – figures not far beyond the capabilities of some 1930s biplanes.

A tricky problem for Brabazon pilots was keeping its wings off the ground. The next largest plane in the world, the B-36 bomber, had a high-mounted wing. But airliners, as everyone knows, have low wings. If the undercarriage had been made long enough to give the required degree of wing-tip clearance the stresses on it would have been too great, and the weight penalty of a strong enough structure prohibitive.

None of these disadvantages deterred the Brabazon com-mittee in 1943 when they sat down to work out what sort of civil airliners Britain should have after the war. The main thing was to show the world that Britain was Great: Britain should therefore have the largest airliner. And 'financial con-siderations must necessarily be secondary'.

The Brabazon was a Great aeroplane. It was also a Great disaster, from the commercial point of view. It never carried a fare-paying passenger. Before long it was found to be suffering from the ailment of metal-fatigue (one of Nevil Shute's *bêtes-noires*). Cracks started to appear round the engines, and analysis showed that most of the structure was only good for 5,000 hours of life. But the whole concept of the Brabazon was becoming unnecessary as more and more airports were extending their runways quite happily to accept the American long-range airliners.

Duncan Sandys was most tactful, as Minister of Supply, in 'mothballing' the Brabazon, breaking the news gently to the public over a period of months. It was a pity he elected to break up the prototype as well, since it was a beautiful monster. The only part of it that now remains is the nose-wheel, which is now in the Science Museum, and which passing small boys could make retract by pushing a button – until the mechanism broke down.

I personally feel no regrets whatsoever over the Bristol Brabazon. It only cost the taxpayer £12.5 million – five shillings a head roughly – and was better value than a cinema seat. The Brabazon was after all a real three-dimensional object, not some flimsy special effect that could only be photographed from one angle. It was also a beautiful piece of engineering, and had a lovely, memorable shape – that curvaceous fuselage, that exquisitely draped fin (all 50 feet of it), so imperceptibly blending into its fairing, that glider-like wing with its discreetly buried engines in their slim nacelles. ... Those intriguing little air-intakes in the leading edge of the wing ... the dreamlike slowness of its flight.... What if they did have to demolish a village at Filton and scrap a new dual carriageway to create this work of art? A Picasso is not created without breaking some eggs, parbleu!

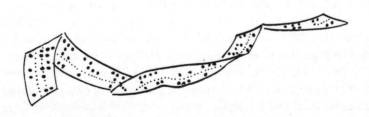

Concorde

OUR PRESENT Great Aerial Flagship is shared, admittedly, with the French, but it too makes use of the facilities at Filton, and our part of it was built by the successors to the Bristol Aeroplane Company – BAC. *Concorde*, as everyone knows, has cost 'X' million (or is it billion?) – that is to say approximately ever-so-much for every man, woman and child in France and England (not forgetting the Channel Islands – or should we call them the Iles Normandes?)

Here again, there has been enormous progress. *Mayfly*, it will be recalled, didn't. R101 did, but shouldn't have. Brabazon did, but Duncan Sandys told us we couldn't afford to let it. *Concorde* does, and we can't afford it, but we can't afford to stop it either.

Concorde's Russian imitator, 'Concordski', was yet more disastrous, blowing up on its first public appearance, in a way that strongly reminds one of R101. A second Concordski was eventually built, but has proved so unsafe and unpleasant to fly that it is only used to carry mail.

The trouble with the Great Aerial Flagships is that two essentially diverse ideas are being confused. The main idea is to have some impressive symbol of national pride and achievement, which employs a lot of people, looks splendid, and does something that has never been done before, or at least not so well, or not for the same reasons. There is a secondary idea, which has somehow become confused with this, which is to transport people from place to place for a reasonable sum. In recent years enormous progress has been made by builders of model aircraft, which grow larger and more beautiful every year. British model builders indeed may be said to lead the world: was not a British team employed for the special effects of the film *Star Wars*? To save the taxpayer from future Concordes I propose that a Government Department be set up to employ a team of model builders on a great British Aerial Flagship. This would be much cheaper, and would leave the field clear for non-disastrous commercial principles to apply to transport.

I have been much inspired in the above reflections by F. W. Hirst's book *The Six Panics*. As an economist, he showed great foresight by condemning the motor-car in 1913, as well as the aeroplane. Far from viewing them as instruments of economic progress hc recognised – and the workers at British Leyland would largely agree with him – that they would mainly be a nuisance.

Bricklin – the Car that Winked

READERS may be familiar with that disastrous motor-car, the Ford Edsel, which appeared in 1957. A fussy-looking machine, with a peculiar oblong radiator intake, it was designed – over-designed indeed – to appeal to the 'upwardly mobile' family. Owners were liable to become upwardly mobile when, as frequently happened, the dashboard caught fire. It was generally easy to get out though, because the door wouldn't close. The car itself gained a reputation for immobility, as the transmission had a habit of seizing up. It was not one of Ford's better-selling models.

More disastrous however, in purely monetary terms, was the Bricklin. This was the brain-child not of any established manufacturer, but of an entrepreneur from Philadelphia named Malcolm Bricklin, who was thirty-five when he proposed the idea to the Government of New Brunswick in Canada. For both parties it was their first and let us hope last attempt at producing automobiles. As well as a total of $20 million in loans the project received moral support from the Conservative Premier Richard Hatfield, who used a prototype to drive around his constituency during the 1974 election. It became a vital element of his campaign to boost the New Brunswick economy. The Bricklin was a hot political issue, and it was Hatfield's baby.

There was a ceremony surrounding the appearance of the first production model from the factory at St John's, and one can only conclude that the car itself was not unaware of the circumstances surrounding its birth. There was much speechifying about 'building a better New Brunswick' and claims that 'this is not just a car'. Then the curvaceous, sporty vehicle, with its gull-wing doors and retractable headlights, and its revolutionary fibreglass-acrylic body, slid smoothly out of the factory doors. One headlight was closed in a conspiratorial wink.

From the start of the venture Malcolm Bricklin showed great flair as a promoter. With unfailing psychological insight, he selected the aspect of the car which he thought would be most likely to sell it to prospective customers. There is a picture of a prototype in the September 1974 issue of *Playboy* magazine, with a fawning covey of bunny-girls. 'The Bricklin has a gutsy, don't-tread-on-me look about it' is the comment. Bricklin's own advertising campaign made the message even clearer: 'Sooner or later', it said, 'you are going to drive a Bricklin, which might prove to be the first great sexual experience of your lifetime'.

This was undoubtedly the only way the car could have been sold, as its appeal as a functional means of transport was limited. The doors were an endless source of problems throughout development, and after a long struggle to get them to raise, close or lock with any degree of reliability, dealers had to advise customers not to drive in the rain, or they would be soaked by the spray coming in from the gaps in the roof. The revolutionary body, made by a process hitherto only tried on lavatory seats, proved impossible to manufacture consistently, and parts of the car would from time to time detach themselves from it unexpectedly. The prototype could not be driven above thirty-five m.p.h. in case its shock-absorbers fell off. During development a unique strength test was devised by the Bricklins. If the moulding survived a blow from a 7 lb hammer it was passed 'O.K.'.

Another novel step was taken by Bricklin's chief designer Herb Grasse, who employed a calendarful of ex-Playmates in the design office at Livonia. This did a lot for morale at Livonia, but since Livonia is in Michigan the workers at the Canadian assembly plant might justifiably have felt somewhat 'left out'. The distance between the various branches of the enterprise contributed enormously to the difficulties of trying to produce a successful vehicle. Most of the components were of Californian manufacture, the design was done in Livonia, Michigan, assembly was in St John and Minto, New Brunswick, financial records were kept in New York, Bricklin's centre of command was in Phoenix, Arizona, and the company's travel bills for the first year came to over $300,000!

It is as a commercial disaster that the Bricklin will best be remembered. Among those who will remember it with peculiar clarity will be the taxpayers of New Brunswick, who have had to pay more than thirty dollars for every man, woman and child in the province. Canadians as a whole have had to provide twelve cents each. The reason for the disaster was that the car simply did not work out as a production-line model: far too much hand labour was needed. Even Malcolm Bricklin admitted that labour costs averaged around $6,300 per car. Since the cars were sold to dealers for $5,400, the outlook for profits was scarcely promising.

In a C.B.C. programme, Prime Minister Hatfield explained that he had this 'gut feeling' about Bricklin. With his responsibility to the people of New Brunswick he had to decide whether the man was just a con-artist or an entrepreneur, and this gut feeling told him Malcolm was the latter. As the St John *Telegraph-Journal* put it: 'So here you have one of the great promotional geniuses of our time, and what he lacks in business acumen, why he makes up in, ah, entrepreneurship.'

The talent of the entrepreneur is to promote, that of the industrialist to produce, and these disparate beings need yet a third talent – that of the manager – to yield good fruit in due season. If any man tells you, dear reader, that he can do all three, and that your money is going to help him to prove it, hold on to your wallet, and remember the Bricklin.

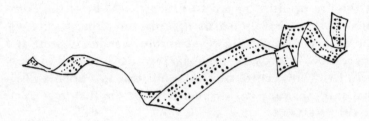

The Mood of Moscow

COMMERCE IS not dead in the Soviet Union, nor is it devoid of disaster, as readers of *Pravda* will know. Where the disasters relate to longer term errors of planning or policy one has to read between the lines to make out what has happened, but smaller scale accidents are frequently aired, and of course there are endless jokes about the whole subject, which tends to be an embarrassing one for Russians.

The worst of all planning disasters was perhaps Stalin's blind faith in the impostor-geneticist Trofim Lysenko, whose theories resulted in many hungry years for the Soviet people. They were still able to joke about it: for instance one wag suggested Lysenko had crossed a giraffe with a cow, resulting in an animal with such a long neck that it could be fed in Hungary while being milked in Moscow. Lysenko would have done well to bear in mind Bernard Shaw's remark to the lady who propositioned him in Zurich on the grounds that he had the greatest brain in the world and she the most beautiful body, so they should produce the most perfect child: 'What if the child inherits my body and your brains?' And when Khruschev embarked on the disastrous attempt to cultivate the Virgin Lands of Kazakhstan in 1954 he would have done well to bear in mind the recent example of the Groundnut Scheme.

Articles appear with great frequency in the Soviet press condemning the twin evils of drink and corruption. Not infrequently the two evils are combined. Plumbers, for instance, are constantly accused of being both drunk and extortionate, and their fondness for bribes is notorious. The activities of plumbers are perhaps a good indicator of the commercial morals of a nation: the client is usually desperate and the plumber footloose and answerable to no one, so where the rules of fair-play in commerce are not respected he is liable to become something of a highwayman.

The Russians have an irrepressible sense of the ridiculous:

an important element in retaining sanity under a totalitarian system. *Krokodil* is full of jokes about themes of daily life such as food shortages.

First Muscovite: 'I queued for two hours today and I still couldn't get any meat. And yet the television is always telling us there are no food shortages, so how is it that there is never anything in my fridge?' *Second Muscovite:* 'Have you tried plugging the fridge into the television?'

Provisioning Moscow

GEORGE DODD, author of *The Food of London*, gives a compendious account of how the capital obtained its supplies in the middle of the nineteenth century. The book has much the same air as Henry Mayhew's *London Labour and the London Poor* published five years earlier. Both these gentlemen convey the feeling of being benevolent Victorian anthropologists adventuring, notebook in hand, through some northern version of an African jungle. Yet one comment of Dodd's about the provisioning of London is as fresh today as in 1856.

'Perhaps the most wonderful characteristic is that – "Nobody does it" – no one assumes the responsibility. It is useless to ask by what central authority, or under what controlling system, is such a city as London supplied with its daily food. "Nobody does it." No one, for instance, took care that a sufficient quantity of food should reach London in 1855, for the supply of two millions and a half of human beings during fifty-two weeks. And yet such a supply *did* reach London.'

In those rare circumstances in which provisions have been supplied by a central authority – the Crimean War, the siege of Paris in 1793 – the results have always been disastrous.

What, I wonder, would Dodd have said about the Soviet Union today. Somehow the State manages to provide for the inhabitants of Moscow ... after a fashion. The State sys-

tem is, however, liable to place intolerable strains upon those
in crucial positions. Michael Binyon, in *The Times*, gives a
tragi-comic account of a housewife who was promoted to
head of the wholesale food distribution section in Moscow.

'She faced a sudden avalanche of bribes and gifts and was
unable to stand the pressure. It ruined her character, her health
and eventually her marriage. The husband, unable to bear

'. . . a sudden avalanche'

the endless round of drinking and revelry, walked out....'

In his account of the failure of the French state to provide for Parisians at the turn of the eighteenth century, Dodd explains that this was because of 'rottenness'. From her husband's description the housewife seems to have suffered from the same form of rot a hundred and eighty years later.

'After her promotion, he said, people began bringing boxes of chocolates to their home. His wife started coming home late – and drunk. "I was invited out", was her answer to his curiosity.

'Indeed she was. The managers of all the shops to which she distributed the produce did their best to ensure their establishments got the pick.

' "Someone from a shop would come with the invoice and bring her salami, a joint of meat, a tin of stew. She used to accept whatever she was given. These she called presents, and I called them bribes", the husband said.

'Her appetite grew. She made a distinction between "her" shops and "others". Whoever did not bring a gift went away without anything. The day was not long enough for her; she was busy looking after "her" shops until late at night, piling up produce from them in her office. Sometimes she bought seventy kilogrammes of salami at once, and similar quantities of meat and tinned produce.

'The presents she received included the traditional bottle of vodka. During business hours the head of the local trade union branch would sit demurely opposite her as though he hardly knew her. But when the client had gone away they would open the gift, have a few swigs and sing and drink until late evening.'

And who is going to blame the poor lady? After all, swigging, singing and making merry are human responses to being the lynch-pin of an inhuman system. The paper *Sovietskaya Rossia* certainly does not blame her unduly: it reserves its especial condemnation for the lady's unfortunate husband, who simply caved in under the pressure. For she gave him, with what must under the circumstances have seemed like a considerable degree of bias, the following view of her position:

'"Everyone round here respects me and that's why they bring me presents. If you don't like it, you can clear out."'

He did – and it would have taken a heroic firmness of purpose to have acted otherwise, in my view. A wife who comes home late, and drunk, and then has the gall to say she is getting free vodka because everyone respects her is beyond the reach of rational persuasion.

'Of all things, an indiscreet tampering with the trade of provisions is the most dangerous; . . . because there is nothing on which the passions of men are so violent, and their judgment so weak, and on which there exists such a multitude of ill-founded prejudices.' So said Burke, and I think he put it rather nicely.

Wheels, Pumps and Sidaroff

A FEW years ago I. Sidaroff, Deputy Director of the Office of Civil Engineering Supplies in Moscow, was ordering materials for an irrigation project in the Kura river valley in Azerbaijan.

Orders of this kind are normally sent by telegram to the factory where the parts are to be made. A telegram was accordingly received at the Karl Marx factory in Tashkent, reading as follows:

REQUEST DELIVERY ONE HUNDRED AND FIFTY TYPE A–Z PUMPS
SOONEST STOP STATE ANTICIPATED DELIVERY DATE – SIDAROFF

The factory, which specialised in making farm carts and parts for tractors, had not so far managed to produce an irrigation pump, though these were on the production plan. The directors met. One honest fellow suggested they should come clean and explain this unfortunate fact.

'What, and be dismissed?' asked his colleagues.

'Well, we could simply ignore the telegram', suggested the Chief Clerk.

'I will ignore that remark,' replied the Managing Director. 'Procrastination didn't get me where I am today. No, I'll show you how to reply: imagination, that's what's needed in a case like this.'

PRODUCTION INITIATED ONE HUNDRED AND FIFTY TYPE A–Z WHEELS DELIVERY THREE WEEKS – KARLMARX FACTORY

The reply came by return:

PLEASE CONFIRM PRODUCTION ONE HUNDRED AND FIFTY TYPE A–Z PUMPS NOT WHEELS – SIDAROFF

Sticking to its guns, the Karl Marx factory replied:

YOUR ORDER TYPE A–Z WHEELS PLEASE SPECIFY RAIL OR AIR FREIGHT – KARLMARX FACTORY

OUR ORDER PUMPS NOT WHEELS AIR FREIGHT IMMEDIATELY – SIDAROFF

YOUR ORDER AIR FREIGHTED AS REQUESTED – KARLMARX FACTORY

This was followed rapidly by:

REGRET YOUR ORDER AIRFREIGHTED TODAY INVOLVED AIR CRASH CARGO BELIEVED STOLEN – KARLMARX FACTORY

But the directors were running out of ideas. As the Managing Director put it, three courses were now open to them: get transferred to another factory, get the production plan changed, or abolish the Ministry.

The Ghost Factory

THE MANAGING DIRECTOR was transferred, I am able
to report, to a tractor factory on the outskirts of Leningrad.
This factory specialised in repairing tractor engines, and was
able to handle fourteen thousand engines a year. The post
was one which evidently required a high degree of imagination in its Managing Director, since the factory, handed over
by the builders in December 1978 and officially opened in
February 1979, did not in fact exist.

Michael Binyon, in *The Times*, explains that although the
project had begun satisfactorily in 1974 it had run into delays.
The State Bank had cut off credit two years later and the
builders had been dismissed. Mr A. V. Prokhorovich, Chairman of Construction Authority No 49, did some imaginative
thinking. They were behind schedule and the prospects
looked bleak. This is not the kind of situation Chairmen like
to admit to, so he decided to get all the construction papers
signed anyway – the actual building could wait. The chief
engineer, who had been replaced in a recent reshuffle, was
signed for by someone else, and the rest followed easily
enough. The fire inspectors could honestly say they had no
fears of fires breaking out in a few trenches full of rubble
and a few half-finished walls. Similarly the Environmental
Protection Agency could certify that there was no pollution
whatsoever emanating from the site.

Unfortunately for Mr Prokhorovich and for our imaginative Managing Director, the independent State auditors were
alerted by reports that the factory was making heavy losses.
Evidently the Managing Director's nerve must have failed,
or he was ignorant of the example of some of the other heroes
of this book, because the first essential in such cases is to produce good healthy figures for profit and turnover. Anyway,
the auditors summoned all those concerned to a meeting, and
several officials were reprimanded, others dismissed.

There are a great many tractors out of action in the collective farms of the north west of Russia, and a great many angry farmers waiting for their engines. There is also a Managing Director looking for a job. I believe we shall hear of him again before long.

Switch Witch

ONE OF the most promising areas for the entrepreneur in Russia today is the manufacture of broomsticks. Brooms are of course essential to everyday life, and there are plenty of birch trees to make them from, according to S. Scherbakov, Chief Forester of the Balashovsky Forestry Cooperative in Saratov. Five years ago this cooperative used to produce over forty thousand broomsticks a year; this number is now reduced to a mere trickle.

Broomsticks are highly labour-intensive. Anyone who has tried tying all those birch switches together round a central pole will appreciate this, and as regulations for night flying get stricter, so a higher standard of broomstick is called for. According to a recent regulation, Russian cooperatives are only allowed to retain twenty-five per cent of profits from industrial production, and to make things worse, only eighteen per cent of expenditure is to be used for labour. Broomstick manufacture is almost all labour, since the basic materials grow on trees. This is why the cooperatives have almost given up making them.

Broomstick prices, predictably, are soaring.

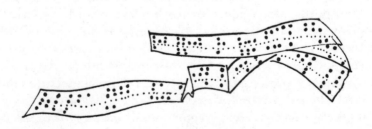

Ballet Shoes

IN AUGUST of 1958 an elderly academician from Moscow
was enjoying his holidays in the mountainous regions of the
valley of the upper Oder, in Poland.

An energetic hiker in spite of his advanced years, he was
relaxing after a bracing walk through forest and meadow in
the foothills just outside Wroclaw. It was a warm evening,
and he sipped gratefully at his iced lager as he sat in a café
in Wroclaw's Rynek Square, watching the citizens of the old
Silesian town hurrying home from work. The air was still,
the sky in the west was a pleasing shade of salmon pink, and
a few bats disported themselves among the eaves of the
colonnade.

He consulted his town guide. That evening he had a seat
at the theatre. 'Wroclaw ... pop. 483,500. Formerly part of
Prussian Silesia, this quaint old town on the banks of the
Oder...' Ah, it was on the next page: 'The Arts. There
are four theatres in Wroclaw, the Pushkin theatre near the
Rynek Square...' It must be that large baroque edifice on
the left. He looked across the square. Not so many people
about now. But what an extraordinary fellow that was,
pirouetting about under the plane trees on the points of his
toes.

He looked more carefully. A lady was advancing towards
the first figure. She too was walking in a curious mincing
fashion, on tiptoe. Suddenly the explanation hit him. It must
be a ballet troupe. How marvellous! In all his years working
for the Ministry of Education he had never forgotten his
youthful passion for the ballet. He would find out where they
were performing, cancel his seat at the theatre – he was in-
wardly shrinking from the thought of an evening struggling
to understand a Polish play – and go to the ballet instead.

Hurriedly summoning the waiter he settled his bill and
strode forth into the square. A young member of the troupe
passed him, also on tiptoe, but contriving to kick a ball as

'. . . in a curious mincing fashion'

he glissaded along. Extraordinary! What talent... so young a performer.... he could not be more than fifteen.

'Excuse me, could you tell me where you are performing tonight?'

'Performing, what do you mean?'

'Aha, you cannot fool me! You, and that lady over there, and that other gentleman, you were practising a routine right on the central *pavé*. I know a *corps de ballet* when I see one!'

'Look, I don't know who you think you are...'

'That's perfectly all right, my dear fellow; I understand, it is an amateur troupe, not part of the overall Cultural Plan.'

'Cultural Plan be damned; it's the five-year plan. Ever since they started rationalising production at the shoe factory, they've only been making shoes in three sizes, one for women, one for children, and one for ... ouch ... men.'

Lord and the Blue Lawn

IT IS not every captain of industry who can boast such fame during his own lifetime as Cyril Lord. Lord started manufacturing textiles shortly after the end of the second world war, and by the time he went public in 1954 his pre-tax profits had topped half a million a year. He embarked on his greatest venture, the manufacture of carpets, three years later, employing copious advertising, vigorous direct sales techniques, and by-passing the wholesaler. By 1966 he was spending nearly £800,000 a year on advertising, much of it through television. In 1967 he was immortalised in the following incident, which occurred in a children's television programme, and is described by A.F.L. Deeson in *Great Company Crashes*:

Batman and Robin were climbing up a skyscraper in pursuit of the Awful Mister Freeze. Near the top of the skyscraper a window flew open, and the familiar face of Cyril Lord appeared.

'Who's that?' Robin asked.

'Why,' answered Batman, 'don't you know, that's the Carpet King of Europe.'

'Holy Matman!' exclaimed Robin.

Fame indeed!

The fall of Cyril Lord's empire says much about the dangers of a large manufacturing business dominated entirely by one forceful personality. By the time the company got into serious trouble in the late sixties Lord's health was beginning to deteriorate, and it was probably a contributing factor in many of the mistakes which were made in these years. Lord loved power boats, of which he had several over the years, all very fast, and all called 'Sea Lord'. When the skill of the man at the helm is everything, his hand must not waver.

It was in 1967 that Cyrilawn was launched, an amazing form of artificial grass. Lord put on a celebrities tennis match at the Hilton in London, featuring Hardy Amies and Barbara

Kelly v. Reginald Maudling and the Marquess of Dufferin
and Ava. Cyrilawn technicians were puzzled when months
after this send-off they found they still had 100,000 square
yards of the material lying unsold. There was of course the
little problem of slime, which some customers found un-
attractive when it formed all over the imitation tufts. Com-
plaints about the grass turning blue in patches could be
countered by pointing out that very soon the green would
disappear altogether, leaving a uniform blue. Surely everyone is aware that there is a perfectly well recognised botanical
variety known as 'blue grass'? Some people, it would seem,
are just impossible to please.

The Last of the Gnomes

THE LIFE of ex-millionaire whizz-kid Colin Stone is the stuff
of legend. The son of a market gardener of modest means,
Colin's first experience of commercial life was selling apples
from a stall. At the age of fifteen he started making fibreglass
garden ponds in his parents' backyard, and before very long
he had sold several of these to neighbours, amassing a hand-
some £500 or so of net profit.

He decided at this point that he had arrived as a successful
businessman. What is the world forum for successful
businessmen? The Chicago Trade Fair. Colin got on a plane
to Chicago with one of his fibreglass ponds. The other stall-
holders at the Fair were so amused at the arrival of this fifteen-
year-old English youth with his funny shaped fibreglass
object that they made a space for him by one of the stands,
and here he set up his wares. Since the purpose of the fibreglass moulding was not particularly obvious, Colin placed
a small garden gnome with a fishing rod at one end. Like
that everyone could see it was a garden pond.

'Gee!' said the Sears Roebuck buyer who happened to be
strolling past. 'What on earth's that thing?'

Gnomes were unknown in America at the time. Colin enlightened the buyer so convincingly as to their nature, habits and role in suburban garden life that he placed a 'trial' order. This was about fifty times as big as Colin could conceivably fill from his supplies.

It was in the mid-sixties and Harold Wilson was Prime Minister. The accent was on export, and there were enormous concessions to be had in the way of credit, factory and employment subsidies and so forth. Gnome manufacturing facilities were set up at record speed; the Sears Roebuck order was followed by many more; and in three years' time Colin found himself a millionaire, being received by Lyndon Johnson at the White House as Young Businessman of the Year.

Before long the original gnome-manufacturing business had expanded to make use of the plastic moulding equipment. Colin's inventive genius turned to traffic markers, boat fenders, even factory chimneys – anything in which plastics could be used. It was a time of rapid expansion in the plastics industry and Colin rode the crest of a wave. The trouble with waves is that they do eventually break, and the inexperienced surfer gets a ducking. Colin's expansive and generous temperament must have made him especially prone to predators, and in 1972 the crash came.

A plastics factory had been set up in the New Territories of Hong Kong, crammed with rotational moulding equipment hastily flown in from America. Alas it was too late. At mid-day on the first day of production the receivers moved in. There had just been time for a test-run of the machinery. The total resultant product of this £400,000 enterprise? One very, very expensive vinyl garden gnome.

The Sally Willey Shoe Spring

NEW INVENTIONS are inherently disaster-prone. The inventor frequently labours for a lifetime without glimpsing commercial success. Mrs Langton (formerly Miss Sally Willey) of Leicester is a prolific female inventor, many of whose ideas have proved most commercial. She has, however, an obsession with footwear. Here her efforts have met with almost unremitting disaster. Thousands of hours of work went into her invention the 'Shoe Spring', for example. Who has not dreamed of bounding along the unyielding asphalt with power-assisted tread? But that was not the idea.

The object of the Sally Willey Shoe Spring was to keep the shoes attached to the feet. Women's shoes may be divided into 'drop-offs', 'right-offs', 'bunion-bags' and 'sideways-gapers' according to Mrs Langton, who takes size 8AAAA. Initial researches were carried out at the Golden Egg Restaurant, Golders Green, the window of which forms an ideal

'... with power-assisted tread?'

83

hide for the foot-watcher. Here Mrs Langton sat, with a co-director of her firm, Schema Ltd, for many happy hours, observing the extraordinary things which happen to feet as they make their way across life's pavements, trapped in deadening encasements of leather, wriggling to free themselves from distorted canvas or parting company at every footfall from flip-flop sandals. Films were then made, from the same vantage point. This research led ultimately to the Shoe Spring, which was tooled up for large-scale production.

With blind stubbornness, the shoe industry has resisted Mrs Langton's efforts at reform. With obsessive perseverance, Mrs Langton has come back at them again and again, at the annual Harrogate Shoe Conference, at Trade Fairs, at orthopaedic institutes. Rejected time after time, and turned away by manufacturer after manufacturer, Mrs Langton has developed a philosophical attitude towards her pet obsession, and has made a collection of manufacturers' excuses for not welcoming her inventions, rather as an unsuccessful novelist papers his walls with rejection slips.

One product (a serviceable-looking little nylon buckle) was rejected as follows:

'Too many colours; too difficult to do up; too easy to undo; too few shades; too large at the back; too short in the knob; too small at the back; the buyer has left; we've moved factory and we threw the samples away; a child couldn't do it up; a mother couldn't do it up; we couldn't do it up; we don't deal with your distributors; we've nothing against it; – and, finally, on a more encouraging note – we like it, but don't tell the manufacturers.'

The Electric Elephant

ANOTHER walking disaster was the all-electric elephant produced for the military as a means of negotiating rough terrain by a leading American electrical manufacturer. The 'elephant' was surmounted by a small howdah in which troops were intended to sit, with suitable armaments.

I was told about this device by a scientist at the Massachusetts Institute of Technology, and I wrote to several leading manufacturers for details of it, but none of them will admit to having invented anything so ludicrous. Military inventions, they reply, would in any case be on the secret list. My own theory is that the creature has got lost: as soon as it realised it had been made, it walked away and is hiding itself for shame.

The 'Boojum' Electric Shark

AN INVENTION of my own which imitates the animal kingdom is the 'Boojum' Shark. Some years ago it was suggested to me by an exiled British 'captain of industry' that there was a great potential market, in our increasingly over-populated and inquisitive world, in devices to protect the privacy of the Very Rich.

This idea immediately appealed to my idealistic instincts, because I have always felt that the Very Rich are among the most luckless and deserving sections of our society. When I see Very Rich people, I think of the grinding misery of their lives, and of the awful dangers they constantly suffer – I have tried to outline some of them in these pages – and my heart warms to them. I am quite serious about this. Apart from the onslaughts on their health produced by excessive consumption of food and drink, their lives cannot be natural in any way. One cannot while away an afternoon picking mushrooms if one knows that as every hour passes a million of one's unblocked Eurodollars are flowing from the Geneva Bourse to the Hong Kong Soft Futures market. Only a very callous man could indulge in mushroom-picking, or in any other normal human pastime, in such circumstances. Then there are endless responsibilities to one's financial managers, one's household staff, the captain of one's yacht, and the man who looks after the racehorses. A life, in short, of relentless duty and intolerable nervous strain.

I therefore designed and built a remote-controlled electric shark, to patrol the beaches where the Very Rich try to take refuge from the pressures of life, and protect their privacy by discouraging the attentions of motorboat-loads full of trippers, photographers and exhibitionistic water-skiers. It was essential to this strategy that the shark should give a life-like impression, but this was easily achieved, since all that one sees of a shark in the water is its fin. Anyway, who ever heard of an artificial shark?

86

When the shark was first tried out on the river Isis, as the Thames is called at Oxford, it met with a challenge which very nearly put paid to it for ever. The trials went very nicely at first, and only a few minor adjustments to ballast were needed. Steering and submersion were satisfactory, and some friends who had come down for a picnic to witness the historic moment cheered as Boojum terrified the moorhens. Roars of laughter went up as a nervous female canoeist took evasive action. This was too much for Sam, the black Labrador, who plunged into the water paddling furiously, leaped on to Boojum and took a bite at his back. My precious creation sank deflated to the bottom of the muddy river. He was fished out several days later by the Oxford Sub-Aqua club, very much the worse for wear.

The effectiveness of Boojum depended entirely on the psychological frame of mind of the observers. No one canoeing or paddling in the Isis could seriously have believed that a shark was likely to be swimming the upper waters of the Thames, so they could hardly have been very alarmed. The model's next test was outside the Royal Southern Yacht Club on the river Hamble, in tidal waters. To add to the realism of the occasion, a friend was persuaded to row up and down in a dinghy, beating at the speeding fin with an oar and uttering piratical curses. This went down much better. A number of yachtsmen on their way down river became quite excited. The next day the rumour was going around in the Club bar that a basking shark had been washed in from the Solent. One choleric old member was heard to mutter, 'Damn river's not safe any more.'

A yet more realistic trial took place in Greece. A shark owner had kindly invited the designer out for a demonstration. Rashly, after a good lunch, I was persuaded to let Boojum go in the harbour of a quiet fishing village. Instantly, a boat was launched, a harpoon brandished, and the entire male population of the village assembled on the quay. The wielder of the harpoon meant business, and evasive action was signalled, bringing Boojum back to safety under water. I then hauled the model, dripping, out of the sea, raised it aloft, grinned and made placatory gestures. This did not work at all. The fishermen had lost face: it was no laughing matter. To prevent a lynching by the crowd of angry Greeks clustering round us the harbourmaster escorted us up to his office. When we ventured out an hour later we found that the fishermen had disappeared, and in their place were gathered the female population, for whom we were heroes. 'Do it again, please do it again!' they cried. We had won a small victory against machoism.

The demand for sharks was curtailed in a very sudden and unexpected way. At the very moment when I was experiencing the events just described, a film company was spending enormous sums on building artificial sharks. Thanks to the film *Jaws* the whole concept of the artificial shark was to become common currency, thereby destroying the credibility of my product. It left me to reflect that had I known of their film or they of my sharks, I should today be the richest special effects man in the business.

The Lonely Strand

ONE OF THE best ways to lose a large sum of money is to invent a new brand of soft drink or a new type of cigarette. People's tastes in these areas are slow to change. A conditioned response has to be learned – like a vital phrase in a foreign tongue – so that the brain, when largely filled with other more fascinating problems, comes up with the right word pattern when prompted by thirst or the need for a smoke. There has to be a certainty that the words, when spoken at the kiosk or the bar, will produce a familiar and pleasant result. No self-respecting adult willingly learns a new pattern of this kind, so most of the population has unalterable habits which advertising is hard put to it to shift.

Nonetheless, the tobacco companies are prone to sudden accessions of restlessness – doubtless the marketing chief needs to prove his worth – and the advertising agencies are delighted to cooperate in those adventurous endeavours: the new brands.

The disasters that result, although colossal by most commercial standards, are shrugged off by industries whose annual turnover is measured in hundreds of millions. Mother dinosaur has stepped on one of her eggs? Never mind, she will lay plenty more, and some of them will grow up to be big dinosaurs one day.

My favourite dinosaur's egg of the tobacco world is the Strand, a Wills cigarette marketed in the nineteen-sixties. 'You're never alone with a Strand' still lingers in the dim

'*Mother dinosaur has stepped on one of her eggs?*'

subconscious hoardings of the back streets of the mind. The lonely figure standing by the Chelsea Embankment in his battered hat and raincoat, watching the festive lighted window across the street – a memorable romantic image. Terence Brook, the actor who performed the commercials, was the perfect embodiment of the disaffected younger generation at whom the advertising was aimed. Innocent yet world-weary, the defiant loser: he bore a striking resemblance to the teenage film hero James Dean. These commercials, invented by a brilliant advertising man called John May, were supposed to capture the mood of loneliness, rejection and defiance which prevailed among young people at the time. This sense of romantic isolation caused them to run in large droves to record shops to buy copies of Frank Sinatra singing 'Only the Lonely', and stampede back to their television sets to watch Johnny Staccato. It was hoped, not unreasonably, that they might find time to pause *en route* to buy a packet or two of Strand cigarettes. The ploy was unsuccessful, probably because with all the jostling at the record counter and the mad scramble to push the rest of the family out of the best seat in front of the television, disaffected youth had forgotten it was supposed to be feeling outcast and solitary. The advertisements made quite an impact ... on Terence Brook's fan mail. Had John May contented himself with making a feature film he would have had a box-office hit. As for the sales statistics, they showed quite an interesting little response among middle-aged childless housewives, who apparently felt motherly towards Terence Brook. No one else very much wanted to buy Strand cigarettes. But Terence Brook became a star.

Up in Smoke

A MISFORTUNE which affected virtually the entire tobacco industry of Great Britain was the introduction of tobacco substitutes. Made from wood pulp, and bearing a close resemblance to cardboard, these substances were believed by the tobacco industry to be less likely to cause lung cancer than the Virginian weed. At this time David Ennals, the Minister for Health, was showing signs of getting tough with the tobacco industry, for which he had little sympathy. Tobacco substitutes might, the industry supposed, be their shield against the threats of repression from the dreaded Ennals. After all, they were safer.

Tests had shown that there were fewer residues from these substitutes after smoking and that the residues themselves were less carcinogenic. All that was necessary was to explain these facts to the public and put the new cigarettes on the market. Unfortunately, the agreement which the Government had with the industry about tobacco advertising made it very difficult to get the message across. The only definition of safety allowed in advertisements was the tar percentage. The tars of tobacco residues are the part which causes cancer; tobacco substitute tar was less carcinogenic than tobacco tar, and although there were fewer residues after smoking, the tar percentage was almost the same. In any case, by this time, genuine tobacco cigarettes were being produced with lower tar yields.

The Department of Health and Social Security Committee on smoking and health, under Dr Robert Hunter (now Lord Hunter of Newington), was consulted. The tobacco industry had gone to all this trouble to produce a safer smoke: surely Mr Ennals would temper the wind to the shorn lamb and modify the advertising rules so as to express the real advantages of the new product? The Committee was unconvinced by this argument. If people were given the impression that the new cigarettes were safer, they would smoke *more*, and it was the Committee's duty to protect the public by persuading them to smoke *less*. In any case, there was only twenty-five per cent of tobacco substitute in the new brands, so any increase in the smoking habit would mean a real worsening of the health hazard. The Committee was also unconvinced by the further plea that this was only a first step towards the real improvement in safety from a hundred per cent tobacco substitute brand. Smoking was a dangerous habit, and the Government was certainly not going to encourage any ideas which were likely to promote it.

The tobacco industry found itself in a 'heads you win, tails I lose' situation. If new brands of tobacco are, like dinosaur eggs, notoriously hard to hatch, the entire dinosaur species had been persuaded in this instance to lay simultaneously. The fear of successful competition made it impossible for any of the leading manufacturers to stay out of the race. It was 'Lay, or perish'. Was the Government lending a hand to evolution and, by engineering a commercial disaster, leading the tobacco industry deliberately towards extinction?

Never can there have been a more difficult marketing campaign. The advertisements were not allowed to state that the product was safer. What about flavour? The flavour of tobacco substitutes, like their appearance, was reminiscent of cardboard. 'Different' was about the most enthusiastic adjective that could be used. The last card was price. Three quarters of the price of a packet of cigarettes is tax. Perhaps, thought some blind optimists, the Government would only tax the tobacco content. After all, they don't tax the filter. Nothing doing. Of the eleven brands which appeared on the market in the summer of 1977 not one was any cheaper than its nearest pure-tobacco rival, and one or two actually cost more, as a reflection of the enormous research and testing costs which had gone into the new material.

Somehow, the new brands had to be sold. After all the fuss, it was too late to back down now. Perhaps the very controversy itself would help – the novelty angle. Seven million pounds were spent on advertising, trying to persuade that conservative figure, the smoker, to change from his favourite brand to a new one which tasted marginally more like cardboard, cost about the same, and was not, according to the advertisements, any safer. He was not impressed.

As Walter Bagehot said of the Overend Gurney crash, a child could have told them what would happen. The losses were punishing. Normally if a new brand fails to 'take', the losses can be offset by repacking the tobacco from a slow-selling batch into the traditional favourites. In the case of tobacco substitutes this was not possible, as the material had been blended in with the tobacco. How then could the stocks of unsold cigarettes be disposed of?

I hope the tobacco industry was right in its contention that tobacco substitutes are safer than ordinary tobacco, because we have all inhaled some in our time. The stocks were burned.

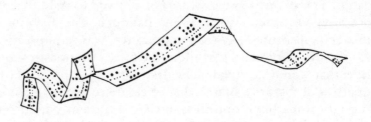

The Pompous Director

ALTHOUGH there are few really well authenticated accounts of leading figures of the commercial world slipping up on banana skins as they descend from their Rolls-Royces, and even fewer of Chairmen experiencing split trouser-seats* as they rise to make after-dinner speeches, the following story from Sir Kenneth Cork has the same deflationary impact.

The unfortunate train of events which caused the near-liquidation of the Coketown Provincial Bank is beyond the scope of this book; however the affair had been handled by Sir Kenneth's firm, Cork, Gully & Co., and it was chiefly remarkable for the off-handed behaviour of one of the directors, who was a Member of Parliament. The man in question had never taken any visible interest in the small bank's affairs, nor had he ever attended a directors' meeting. His name had been included as an ornament. He was, however, obliged to attend when liquidation seemed imminent, though he took great pains to appear as Olympian as possible to the heavy-booted Northerners who constituted the bank's working directors.

Some years later Mr Cork, as he then was, was sailing in Brittany when it was decided to put in at Deauville. It was 'La Grande Semaine', and the delights of the season included polo as well as racing. Having negotiated the lock and tied up, the members of the crew, including Mr Cork, lost no time in going ashore, the first port of call being the bar of Deauville Yacht Club.

Normal male attire when sailing is canvas trousers (usually a dull brick colour) or jeans, an open-necked shirt, and an all-purpose navy jacket whch spends most of the voyage rolled up in a ball in some recess of the boat. This is dug out and given a couple of shakes before being slipped on to 'smarten up' when going ashore.

*Stop Press: Sir Robert Lusty, a Chairman many times over, reports (*The Times*, 4 June 1980) a crucial failure of the trouser braces in the Ritz Foyer. Does this mark the onset of a new outbreak of trouser catastrophes?

The voyage had been a little rough, and the party were still wearing their sea-boots when they joyously made their way along the quay to the clubhouse. On entering the bar Cork was hailed by a friend.

'Kenneth, old chap, you look as though you could do with a drink.' Then, turning to an immaculately suited figure standing next to him, who was surveying the bar with an Olympian air. 'Oh, I wonder if you know Sir Blankety-Blank M.P. This is Mr Kenneth Cork.'

'Yes, I think we've met before.'

'I doubt it.' (This with a sneering glance at the sea-boots and the salt-stained trousers).

'I do believe we have, sir.' Since the M.P. rudely made no reply, but clearly implied that he was not in the habit of mixing with scruffy sailors called Cork, the temptation was too great. . . .

'Oh, don't you remember, it was when you were going bust!'

Primrose and the Plank

THE SPORT of sailing is a commercial disaster for the devotee – it has been compared to standing in the fountains of Trafalgar Square in a Savile Row suit tearing up banknotes.

Those who supply the yachts and all those beautiful gadgets which adorn them do not generally fare so badly. However, accidents do happen, and yacht designer Angus Primrose tells the following spine-chilling story of the fate that awaits a designer who takes his calculations one step too far.

One raw evening in October, Angus Primrose arrived at a small yacht club on the West Coast of Scotland to dine with the owner of a forty-eight-foot sloop he had designed. The yacht was a racy modern vessel with a rather narrow beam, a reversal of the trend of recent years. He had great hopes for it, and if successful it was to be the prototype for a production run of expensive cruisers which were to be built by a famous firm in the Solent. Trials were to be held the following day, and assuming all went well, the owner hoped to start on a world cruise before the weather got too bad.

The bar was a fine old room, a little dark perhaps, with a lot of polished brass and shining mahogany, and large sombre leather chairs. The walls were decorated with the usual photographs of billowing canvas and brave lads hauling at the sheets; there was a large wooden tablet with the names of former Commodores painted on it, and there was a particularly splendid set of those wooden half-mouldings of yacht hulls, with names underneath in gold lettering.

The owner had not yet arrived, so the designer settled himself in one of the chairs and started looking through a list of the points he wanted to check during the trials. Before long, he became aware of a gentle coughing sound at his shoulder. Looking round he beheld a very old gentleman in a wing collar with bleary eyes and a Max Beerbohm moustache: the type of Edwardian face normally accompanied by a straw boater.

'Ah hope ye'll parrdon the intrusion, but are ye no Angus Primrose, the designer?'

'Yes.'

'So you're the laddie that designs those fine racing yachts for the Admiral's Cup at Cowes, am I right?'

'Well, some of them.'

'Just so, just so. We dinna get a lot of designers calling at the club the noo, ye understand.'

'Er, no.' (What was the old palterer driving at?)

'Ah just thought mebbe ye'd like to know, that's the Designer's Chair ye're sitting in ... aye, the one he sat in the night afore ...' The old man's voice trailed away and his eyes grew glaucous. He laid a skinny hand on Primrose's arm. 'Just come over here, laddie....'

There, in a dark recess, round the corner from the bar, was a half-moulding of a yacht of astonishingly racy lines. So racy in fact that, as he drew closer, Primrose realised that the designer, in an all-out quest for speed, had reduced the beam to the point where the hull was a mere vertical plank, knifing its way through the waves. 'Yacht *Mayfly* – 1907 – Length: 48ft, draught: 8ft, beam: 5ft' ran the inscription, and below this 'Sank with all hands, including the designer, on her maiden voyage.'

Just next to the model there was a yellowing photograph of the *Mayfly*, moored to the quay below the clubhouse, with a group of elegantly attired bewhiskered gentlemen admiring her lines. Would that be the designer, he wondered, in the middle of the group – with a straw boater and a Max Beerbohm moustache.... He spun round. The old man had vanished. But on the far side of the room he espied the owner, at last, waving a hand and advancing towards him.

'What will you have, Angus?'

'A very large Scotch if you please, in a nice *broad* tumbler, and *no water*.'

(*Note: It was with great regret that the author and publishers heard of Angus Primrose's tragic death at sea, shortly before the third impression of this book went to press.*)

Jacob's Well

THE JACOBS have been established in New York for many generations. Their ancestors fought in the crusades, and there is a tomb commemorating the fact in Chale Abbey, Isle of Wight. A more recent ancestor bought a considerable slice of Manhattan Island for a case of gin, and thanks to this purchase the Jacobs were able in subsequent years to insulate themselves against the more sordid preoccupations of commercial life.

Walter Jacob lived at the turn of the century, when the proper business of a gentleman was sport, not commerce; indeed as his wife used to say to her grandchildren – one of whom told me this story – 'money is not a subject one discusses'. As Walter had a weak chest his doctors advised him to try the sun and fresh air of Texas. The family moved down to a ranch outside San Antonio, where they built a big rambling house with a good many balconies and a lot of wooden clapboard fretted into elegant shapes, and verandas, and a fine vista over a lake, where they could picnic and row about in straw boaters, looking very charming and Edwardian. There were many acres round the building, in which sheep and cattle grazed, and there was plenty of land for riding and shooting. It was a pleasant, countrified part of the world.

Until, that is, the bustling fellow with the attaché case arrived on the scene. It appears that he was hoping to buy some of Walter Jacob's land. Walter was quite taken aback. He had none to sell: the ranch was just fine the size it was now. The man didn't seem to understand, and Walter had to be quite blunt with him before he would go away. In a few days' time, in spite of this rebuttal, he showed up again. This time he was rattling on about leaseholds and reversions and the Lord knows what. Walter Jacob grew really annoyed and asked him to please leave, as he had a sick mare to attend to, and he had no time to listen to such stuff.

The next day another man arrived, rather better dressed and riding a decent horse. It turned out that he was an associate of the first man. He was much better spoken and he apologised to Mr Jacob for his colleague's brash behaviour. Walter was feeling somewhat contrite about the way he had behaved to the fellow with the attaché case (it had been a white lie about the mare), so he explained very politely to this new visitor that he had to have the grazing land for the sheep and cattle, and the ranch would be too small if he sold any; besides, he liked plenty of space around him – this was why he'd come to Texas. The new visitor was most affable. He smiled ingratiatingly, complimented Mr Jacob on his choice of land and said he thought the lake very picturesque. Really all he and his friends wanted was to look for minerals, and if Mr Jacob would sell them a concession on the mineral

rights he promised they would not interfere with the grazing.

Minerals. Walter remembered the glass cases in the Natural History Museum, and fossil hunters with little hammers. He felt quite abashed. Of course they could have the mineral rights. By great luck the man happened to have a contract on him, and the terms really seemed most generous to the Jacob family.

The contract was signed, and with renewed assurances about the protection of the grazing, the man rode away.

One hundred and sixty-eight of the richest oil wells in Texas were sunk in that grazing land. Walter died not long after – before the derricks had altogether ruined the landscape. His family sold the ranch in the end, for very little, since by this time it was not exactly a prime residential site. Before leaving they did manage to sink an oil well of sorts, and they kept the rights to this one. It did produce – indeed it yields them an income to this day – though not a very large one, for it has to share the oil with the other one hundred and sixty-seven. Mrs Jacob was right. Money is not a subject for gentlemen.

The Mamelon of Dandenong

THERE IS no doubt that land can be an extraordinarily good investment, especially if someone decides to build one of the world's largest cities on it a few years after you have bought it. Nevertheless, unexpected snags do crop up, and the landowner should always be on his guard against ingratiating visitors with contracts in their attaché cases. In Melbourne, Australia, in 1972, a piece of land came onto the market which seemed like an excellent speculation. It was a small dairy farm of ninety-six acres on the edge of an industrial zone called Dandenong, and it was right next to the General Motors Factory. When the land was zoned as an industrial area the farmer decided to sell up and found a willing purchaser at $275,000. The farmer made arrangements to lease back the grazing rights until such time as the builders moved in.

The purchaser soon became aware of a problem which arose from the local topography. To start with, the land was low-lying and prone to flooding; moreover, it was very uneven – in fact there was a notable mamelon or hillock in the centre, surmounted by a small clump of trees. This was a favourite place for cows to congregate, as it kept their hooves dry in winter, and they were able to keep cool in the summer in the shade of the trees.

The purchaser decided – indeed the suggestion came from the farmer – that a good way to solve this problem would be to bulldoze down the hump and spread the soil over the low-lying land in order to raise it and reduce the danger of flooding. Since such a project was beyond his scope he resolved, rather than developing the land himself, to sell it to a third party, explaining the situation but pointing out the excellent position of the land and its enormous potential value. A buyer was found for $750,000.

This buyer, an expert in land reclamation, soon calculated that the volume of the hillock, spread over the ninety-six acres, would raise the level of the land no more than a few inches, which would be insufficient to prevent the annual floods. As he was a clever man, and the market was buoyant, he was able to sell again within a very short space of time, for a cool $1,950,000, to a fourth party, who then went bankrupt.

Unaware of the rocketing value of the land on which they stood, the cows grazed on. As I write, they are still munching away.

'... a favourite place for cows'

The Whole of the Assets

LET US end this discussion of land values on a more positive note, with a liquidation presided over by the accountants Cork, Gully & Co. In this incident a firm of brick manufacturers was being wound up. Their operations had been carried out upon a depressing piece of land cluttered with derelict buildings and corrugated iron shacks. The principal feature of the landscape was an enormous excavation surrounded with heaps of grey slag, to which a few weeds clung forlornly. Apart from the land itself, which even the most eulogistic estate agent could hardly have described as 'desirable', the main assets consisted of a few pieces of machinery and assorted heaps of rusty metal, and it looked as though the creditors were going to get about twopence in the pound. There seemed no way in which the liquidators could improve the position until one evening at a dinner given by a member of the town's business community they met a local councillor. Over the port a deal was hatched which enabled the creditors to be repaid very nearly in full. The site's most valuable asset had been overlooked. It was something the Local Authority urgently needed: a place to bury refuse. And there it was, in superbly appropriate surroundings – one highly desirable, giant-economy-size hole in the ground!

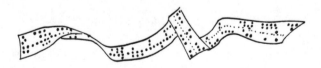

Plummeting Stockbrokers

IT IS SAID that the scene depicted on the cover of this book rarely, if ever, occurred. J. K. Galbraith strongly contests the myth in his book *The Great Crash, 1929*, saying that it was mere cheap journalistic hyperbole. There were suicides at this time, statistically about the usual number, and of course some were attributed to the market crash. There were people who jumped out of windows, though not very many, and there is no single recorded case of a stockbroker behaving in such a manner, according to Galbraith.

The following, however, is an eye-witness account which puts the record straight. I know it must be true because it was told to me by my friend Mr Robert Levinsky, formerly a Wall Street broker, and now a writer of children's books – principally about fish.

Levinsky occupied a thirtieth floor office not a stone's throw from Wall Street, and in the opposite block, but on the fortieth floor, lived his old friend and rival Weinstock, also a broker.

One day as Levinsky was busying himself with some Preferred Bonds he happened, in a quiet moment, to hear a loud cry and a whooshing sound. He looked out of the window. It was Weinstock, diving headlong for *terra firma*.

'I wonder what he knows that we don't,' he remembers saying at the time.

I am sure that Levinsky would not tell this story about himself if it were not true. It is after all not a very nice thing to have said about an old friend – albeit a rival – at such a critical moment.

The stock market does have a powerful effect on people's emotions, of course, and it is no use having a rational approach to it. There is nothing worse than a rational investment policy in an irrational world. 'Adam Smith', the pseudonymous author of *The Money Game*, gives an account of a psychiatrist with the perfect answer to the whole business of stock market investment. The psychiatrist was an alarmingly rational man, and he had found the perfect stock. It was so good that he held just the one – all others being of inferior worth. He was the sort of man who made you feel about two feet tall as he spoke to you. His choice of stock was based, he explained, on an infallible knowledge of human nature, and he was writing a book about the Stock Market and the Human Mind. 'Adam Smith' asked him if he could outline, very briefly, one or two of his findings. No, he most certainly would not: did 'Adam Smith' imagine he was going to summarise the carefully garnered lore of a lifetime's study and observation in a few glib sentences?

The psychiatrist did, however, go so far as to reveal the name of the stock, which was Westec – indeed he urged 'Adam Smith' to buy some. It had gone from 5 to 10. That was when he had bought in, and since then it had motored up to 30, but it was sure to reach 200. 'Adam Smith' was duly sceptical. There was something he 'just couldn't get with' – the earnings seemed 'stuck together somehow'.

Predictably, the psychiatrist came a cropper. The stock reached 60; then trading was suspended; then the company went bankrupt. 'Adam Smith's' hunch had been right. As for the psychiatrist, presumably his now thoroughly discredited recipe for success would be revealed if his publishers still wanted to publish his book.

This is referred to as a 'happy ending'. I suppose it all depends whose point of view you take. I must say, for all his intimidating behaviour and know-all air, I feel a little sorry for the psychiatrist, who, the author recounts gleefully, had picked up the one stock that permitted him to lose not merely a lot, but everything. I read on eagerly at this point to see if the psychiatrist was going to jump out of a window. It doesn't say if he did, though we are rather left to assume that something of the kind must have occurred. Anyway, 'Adam Smith' was right and the psychiatrist was wrong, which makes it a fifty per cent happy ending.

Anyone who is too depressed by this display of effortless superiority on 'Adam Smith's' part may be interested to know that the pseudonym – the book goes on at some length about why he chose it – conceals the identity of George J. W. Goodman. Yes, ladies and gentlemen, there he is in the fourth row – the editor of the *Institutional Investor* who organised a famous conference once, for a great figure of the investment world. Mr Goodman was the man who gave you, on the 4th of February 1970, that great performer, none other than the unique, the world renowned – Mister Bernie Cornfeld! (Loud applause.) And then, one year later, after the biggest Investment Trust crash of all time, Mr Goodman invited him back, and this time the title of his speech was: 'What went wrong?' (Commotion in the fourth row.)

Mr Goodman too deserves some of our sympathy.

Disastrous Names II

ANY DISCUSSION of this topic is incomplete without a mention of Introductions Ltd, a British company formed a few years after the war to extend the benefits of pig farming to the general public. The subscriber to Introductions was introduced, as it were, to a pig, who then bore his name on an ear tag. The introductions were not a social success, nor a financial one, and the company went into liquidation. One irate shareholder insisted on claiming her own pig, and arrived on the scene accompanied by a policeman, who then volunteered to search through the assembled animals to find one bearing her name. This proved harder than he had bargained for, and the pigs took concerted action against him. Exit policeman pursued by pigs.

I am not maintaining that the name has more than a marginal effect on the fate of a company – but a form of poetic justice operates, often quite capriciously: if for instance you call a company 'Unexcelled' you may well find that Aubrey McFate makes you an unexcelled disaster. This happened to Unexcelled N.V., Curaçao, through which I.O.S. lost such a lot of money. Grandiose names such as 'Global Enterprises' are also prone to deflation by whichever heavenly department it is that levies the vanity tax. Very small and dubious firms dealing in cheap air travel or 'import and export' tend frequently to have high-sounding names. Be warned: the bigger the façade, the bouncier the cheques.

Since this is not a history book I have not described the collapse of the South Sea Bubble. I must say I would not, however, have chosen the name 'South Sea Bubble Knitwear' for a firm which made sweaters. A soggy woollen bubble does not sound likely to remain afloat for very long – nor did it. Another curiously preposterous name which is no longer with us is that of the Wapping Egg Breaking Company. In the interests of commerce, apparently, eggs have to be broken, though one would have thought that the manufacturers of dried egg and other foods would have been able to do this for themselves: perhaps they have now learned to.

When it was announced that the last of the Lyons tea shops were to close there was a great deal of correspondence in the press concerning the possible influence of the recently adopted name 'Jolyon' in hastening their demise. Jolyon – the name of characters in the Forsyte Saga – was held to be too unlike the original 'Joe Lyons' for the average customer to make the connection. Though I am inclined to agree that Jolyon was an awkward substitute for the familiar original, what the correspondence really reveals is the degree of attachment the public forms to stalwart old favourites. The teashop chain had really started to decline during the second world war, when about 70 of the original 240 or so shops were destroyed. They became increasingly less economic, and were closed down at a steady rate as labour became more expensive, and the properties they occupied grew more valuable. The change of name may have been a blow to the nostalgic, but it neither hastened nor reduced the rate of closure of the teashops. Perhaps nostalgia should be itemised in 'goodwill' calculations. There must have been a lot of it going for Joe Lyons, to judge by the reaction to the closure of the last cafés, for by the time it was announced there were only fifteen left.

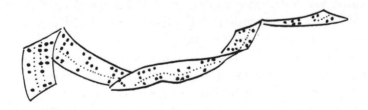

De Angelis and the Phantom Oil

EDIBLE oils play a major role in the commodities market, where one deals with that least tangible of all assets: the future. This lends a strange, ghostly air to the whole business. One wonders, for instance, where those pork bellies – a favourite with commodity speculators – will be in three months, when they are 'due', and for that matter, what about the rest of the animals? Will they have dematerialised?

For the great Tino de Angelis, the border-line between reality and myth was slightly nearer to the myth side than it is for most of us. He has been labelled as a swindler, but my feeling is that he was a sort of Conan Doyle: a man whose enormous imaginative powers enabled him to build up a monumental *œuvre*, but led him in later years to become somewhat obsessed with psychical research. The phantom in this instance was not some disembodied spirit, but crude vegetable edible oil.

Short and round in outward appearance, de Angelis was a giant in all other respects. Before going on to greater things he wisely built up a sound record of achievement in hog-dressing. This was a good solid start, rather as an operatic tenor might master '*Funiculi, funicula*' before going on to the more fancy stuff.

The centrepiece of his later repertoire was none other than the Allied Crude Vegetable Oil Refining Corporation Inc. (Allied for short, alas too short ...). He founded this firm in 1955, by which time this Caruso of Salad Oil was barely forty, and a millionaire several times over.

Starting, like all great entrepreneurs, from modest surroundings (in the Bronx), he was later able to claim that 'No one in the world ever did more for the economy of this country than I did.' This was because he had the true entrepreneur's understanding of money: the realisation that money is no more than a cipher, an almost imaginary substance that only becomes real when circulated. It was as a circulator of money that de Angelis performed his greatest services to the United States: just a small example was his skill with the Petty Cash. During his last and greatest four months of operation – before the paper whirlwind was reaped by the Produce Exchange – the flow of Petty Cash amounted to $458,000. Let us pause in awe before that figure. A dashing way with the Petty Cash is the mark of the stylist in commerce: a sign of imagination and flair. But over $110,000 a month elevates the whole concept of Petty Cash to a higher plane. It is no longer 'Petty'. This sort of trail-blazing alone must have done no end of good to American commercial thinking.

'... the flow of Petty Cash amounted to $458,000.'

De Angelis came from a close-knit family, and believed in family solidarity. He had nothing, however, to do with the Family (Cosa Nostra), though, coincidentally, a partner in one company was Herman Topel. Topel had been front man for Sam ('Teetz') Battaglia, Marshall Caifano, Obbie Frabotta and Leo 'The Mouse' Rugendorf.

The family (small 'f') atmosphere at Allied was important. There was Leo Bracconeri, the plant manager, who was Tino's brother-in-law. There was Ben Rotello, financial controller, who was like a brother. There was George Bitter, who, as Tino was fond of saying, was like a father, and was a trader as well as being the chauffeur. There was Alfredo Suarez, who signed the cheques, and was like an uncle. And, in various less essential capacities there were Michael de Angelis, Louis de Angelis, Thomas de Angelis, Anthony de Angelis and two Dominic de Angelis's. There was a very lovely family atmosphere of loyalty and mutual cooperation among these henchmen. Tino was a very appreciative boss. There were $400-a-week salaries, regular gifts of Cadillacs, and occasional cash payments of $10,000 or so. But more important to the *esprit de corps* was Tino's appreciation of their work.

Take Alfredo Suarez, the deeply tanned, silver-haired Cuban emigré who held the important position of chief financial officer – Ben Rotello's boss. Tino was touchingly enthusiastic about his work. 'You have never seen anything more beautiful in your life than Alfredo Suarez's books.' Nor, as it transpired, had Alfredo himself: he later testified that he hadn't seen the books at all for the past two years. He had, however, a remarkable signature, a sort of Caribbean version of Elizabeth the First's, with which, when asked, he would decorate Ben Rotello's papers. One can imagine him during the long hours in the office, deprived of his precious books, practising that signature and dreaming nostalgically of the good old days in pre-Castro Cuba. He would never have probed indelicately into the affairs of those who knew more about the company than he did; in any case, his English was not too good. So he contented himself with developing a really fine version of the signature for permanent incorporation into a cheque-printing machine. The fifty or so leading banks, from the Chase Manhattan to the Société Générale de Paris, who later found themselves entangled in the demise of Allied, must have greatly valued the artistic qualities of that signature. Perhaps they have framed it and attached it to their office walls, like pre-Revolutionary Russian Railway Bonds: a collector's prize? *Sicut flos inter spinas* – thus blooms art amid the weeds of the market-place.

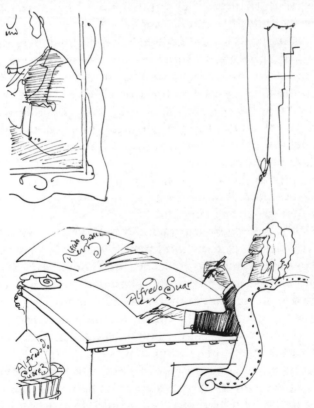

'... practising that signature'

De Angelis's plans for Allied were on the grand scale. Over the years he had built up a considerable international trade, starting shortly after the war, when he had visited Yugoslavia. Appalled by the poverty of the inhabitants, queueing in the streets for food, he had arranged for a group of American businessmen to sell Yugoslavia a million dollars' worth of lard on a year's free credit. Due no doubt to shipping delays the lard was bad when it reached Yugoslavia, and the ungrateful Government sued him. Generously, he settled their claim with $100,000.

This experience stood him in good stead six years later, when the Agriculture Department sued him over nineteen million pounds of smoked meat which his company, Gobel Co., had supplied for the Federal School Lunch Programme. All he had done was to short-circuit a Government inspection; the delay might have caused the meat to go off, and as a family man, who was fond of children, he would not have had that happen for the world. This cost him the permanent displeasure of the Agriculture Department, though he appeased their claim, for the moment, with another $100,000 payment.

De Angelis became a supplier of oil to the United Kingdom, India, Pakistan, Egypt and Yugoslavia. It was in Spain that he met his match.

By 1961, Allied's storage facilities in Bayonne, New Jersey, were the largest of their kind in the world. Enormous silos stood in ranks along the dockside, interconnected by a maze of pipes and pumping stations. These tanks had in fact been designed to store crude mineral oil, but had been most carefully converted, as I shall explain, for their new purpose.

De Angelis was spending much of his time abroad. The centre of his operations in Spain was the Castellana Hilton. From this base he had just negotiated the biggest ever sale of oil to the Spanish Government – for $36.5 million. Obviously there would be those who would be jealous of success on such a scale. Apart from his old enemy, the Agriculture

Department, there were the Big Oil Crushers. Now I, and I am sure my readers, would think twice before doing anything to incur the displeasure of the Big Oil Crushers. Big Oil Crushers are not the people to fool around with. But one would not perhaps have suspected them of cunning – let alone of being the type to link their cause with that most terrible and secret organisation: the Opus Dei. To many of us, the Opus Dei, a Catholic lay association whose members aim to give Christian witness in their everyday work, might seem no more terrible than the Agriculture Department, but in De Angelis's mind it sowed the seeds (rape? cotton?) of Allied's undoing, and it did so at the behest of the Big Oil Crushers.

A late night visit to the Castellana Hilton by an Opus Dei agent tipped him off. Unless he capitulated and renounced the contract, he would never sell another pound of oil to Spain. To many of us it might seem that this 'agent' had merely voiced the opinion that Spain had better things to do with $36.5 million than buy American salad oil.

Meanwhile, in an entirely logical move, de Angelis had begun to buy salad oil futures in a big way. Certain in his mind of the success of the Spanish deal, he was sure that the price of oil would rise, and he would need more oil in any case to fill the order.

At this point, however, logic began to take a secondary role, and grandeur of vision took over. To have sold the oil futures just because this particular deal had fallen through would have been to incur large short-term losses. But more than this, it would have meant an admission of defeat. Like the gambler on a losing streak, de Angelis would not back down, and he began to deal more and more heavily in commodity futures. Rumours of deals, Agriculture Department crop predictions, crop failures in the Ukraine, Egyptian deals, Indian deals, Indonesian deals swam into view and vanished again at an increasingly hectic pace as de Angelis committed himself ever more deeply to the future of the soybean and the cottonseed. The further he got in the more unthinkable it became to retreat: by October 1963 a one per cent drop in prices would have meant having to find $13,560,000 in twenty-four hours. By this time over three quarters of the cottonseed futures on the U.S. Produce Exchange were held by Allied. And during the period 30 August–27 September 1963 his warehouse receipts, by which the commodity dealing was financed, amounted to 937 million pounds of oil, roughly equal to the U.S. Census Bureau's calculation of the entire oil crop of the country.

It is in my view not possible to dismiss de Angelis simply as a swindler. He had risen by means of hard work and intelligent innovation to a leading position in the commercial world. And at every step he had been supported by some of the most reputable institutions of that world. In the words of Kamerman, a partner of Haupt, Allied's commodity dealers: 'De Angelis had been in this business a long time. He was the dominant factor in it. The bankers had seen his plant and liked it very much.' Nevertheless it is at this point that the credulity of the faithful becomes strained.

The warehouse receipts, on the strength of which he was able to borrow money for his commodity trading, were issued by the American Express Field Warehousing Company. This company employed an inspector, who would periodically order that a sampling device be dropped from the top of each tank to the bottom, to record its contents. Invariably, the tanks were found to be full of oil. How should one explain the fact that, when Allied was finally declared bankrupt, and a tap was opened at the bottom of the tanks, salt water poured out for twelve days?

It was simple: a tube had been welded in, exactly beneath the sampling hatch. This tube was full of good salad oil. The rest of the tank was full of water. The other access plates were rusted up and could not be opened. Who could have thought of such a thing? Who could have hit upon the idea of claiming that forty tanks were in operation when there were only ten? Who could have issued forged American Express receipts for 395 million pounds of oil? Could this be tubby, family man Tino de Angelis, with his record of achievement in hog-dressing, his philanthropic work for Yugoslavia, his concern for American schoolchildren?

The repercussions of de Angelis's activities were enormous. Losses suffered by the commodity brokers Haupt and the American Express Field Warehousing Company, rebounding along the chain of exporting companies, banks, and other institutions of commerce, amounted to over $200 million. Haupt was liquidated, the U.S. Produce Exchange was forced to close for a day, and American Express shares dropped thirty per cent, and did not recover for many years.

It is tempting to wish that the Agriculture Department had been more successful in its 'vendetta' or that Opus Dei had stepped in sooner. But reform would have been better than a crash. The real culprits must be those financial institutions whose greed to get their hands on some of the money that poured from Caruso de Angelis's magic Cruse of Oil enabled them to overlook the tell-tale signs of sloppy accounting, past bankruptcies and fraud suits which were staring them in the face.

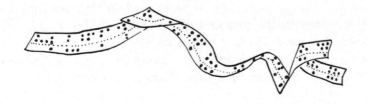

Disastrous Names III

BRAINS' FROZEN FOODS have adopted the following slogan for their pork meat balls, in defiance, presumably, of American susceptibilities (or perhaps to arouse American minority interests?): 'Faggots. Great Balls of Goodness. Pork Faggots from Brains' Frozen Foods'.

A prominent company, when introducing a new frozen cod package, chose the name 'Battered Cod Pieces' until it was pointed out to them what painful implications this might have for Shakespearean actors.

A Toast to Success

Let us conclude this chapter of accidents with a libation to the gods of success. What could be fitter for the purpose than a stein of foaming Loewenbrau, for, in the words of a recent advertisement: 'Not a single bottle gets the Loewenbrau label until the brew has been tasted and passed by a panel of German beer experts.' Well, on second thoughts, perhaps not. How about something more potent – a Hennessy cognac for instance. The reasons for the phenomenal success of this drink in the Far East (and the embarrassed giggles of Japanese ladies when the bottle is produced after dinner) are now known. I cannot divulge them here without indelicacy, but they are connected with the potent little symbol of the 'bras armé' (the mailed clenched fist) which adorns every bottle. What, after all, could be more popular among the Japanese business community than an alcoholic French aphrodisiac? So – a Hennessy please, waiter, and here's to success!

ACKNOWLEDGEMENTS

I should like to thank the following people who helped me with this book. This does not in any way imply that they are more disaster-prone than anyone else – indeed they are demonstrably less so, for at least they have a sense of humour. Jeffrey Archer; Tim Bell; Donough O'Brien; Edward Bourne; Sir Kenneth Cork G.B.E.; Mrs Polly Drysdale; Monique and Maurice Baird-Smith; Michael Ivens; Dr Max Hartwell; David Nye; Mrs Sally Langton; James Evans; J. R. Jordan; Dr Steven Lukes; Dmitri Negroponte; Angus Primrose; Geoffrey Robinson M.P.; N. L. Salmon; Colin Stone; Colin Simpson; Professor A. Nove; Peter Udell; Brian Widlake.

SOURCES

The Times

Euromoney Magazine

The Old Lady – the staff magazine of the Bank of England

Fortune

Newsweek

Deeson, A. F. L., *Great Company Crashes*, Foulsham 1972

Fredericks, H. A. with Chambers, Alan, *Bricklin*, Brunswick Press 1977

Frischauer, Willi, *Onassis*, Bodley Head 1968

Hirst, F. W., *The Six Panics and Other Essays*, Methuen 1913

Kindleberger, Charles Poor, *Manias, Panics and Crashes*, Macmillan 1978

Miller, Norman C., *The Great Salad Oil Swindle*, Gollancz 1966

Gilbert, James, *The World's Worst Aircraft*, M & J Hobbs and Michael Joseph 1975

Raw, Charles, Hodgson, Godfrey, Page, Bruce, *Do You Sincerely Want to be Rich?*, André Deutsch 1971

Shaplen, Robert, *Kreuger, Genius and Swindler*, André Deutsch 1961

Shute, Nevil, *Slide Rule*, Heinemann 1954

'Smith, Adam', *The Money Game*, Michael Joseph 1968

Wood, Alan, *The Groundnut Affair*, Bodley Head 1950